Edward Dowden

Shakespeare

Edward Dowden

Shakespeare

ISBN/EAN: 9783337063443

Printed in Europe, USA, Canada, Australia, Japan

Cover: Foto ©Thomas Meinert / pixelio.de

More available books at **www.hansebooks.com**

Literature Primers.

Edited by JOHN RICHARD GREEN, M.A.

SHAKSPERE.

BY

EDWARD DOWDEN, LL.D.

PROFESSOR OF ENGLISH LITERATURE IN THE UNIVERSITY OF DUBLIN,
AUTHOR OF "SHAKSPERE, HIS MIND AND ART; A CRITICAL STUDY."

NEW EDITION.

London:
MACMILLAN AND CO.

[*The Right of Translation and Reproduction is Reserved.*]

CONTENTS.

CHAPTER I.
THE ELIZABETHAN DRAMA . . . . PAGE 5

CHAPTER II.
SHAKSPERE'S LIFE 13

CHAPTER III.
EARLY EDITIONS OF SHAKSPERE'S WRITINGS . . 30

CHAPTER IV.
EVIDENCE OF THE CHRONOLOGY OF SHAKSPERE'S WRITINGS 32

CHAPTER V.
PERIODS OF SHAKSPERE'S CAREER: GROUPS AND DATES OF PLAYS 47

CHAPTER VI.
INTRODUCTIONS TO THE PLAYS AND POEMS.

	PAGE		PAGE
Titus Andronicus	61	The Phœnix and the Turtle	111
King Henry VI. Part I.	62	The Sonnets	112
Love's Labour's Lost	63	Twelfth Night	114
The Comedy of Errors	65	Julius Cæsar	117
The Two Gentlemen of Verona	68	Hamlet	119
A Midsummer Night's Dream	70	All's Well that Ends Well	123
King Henry VI. Parts II. & III.	74	Measure for Measure	125
King Richard III.	78	Troilus and Cressida	127
Venus and Adonis	80	Othello	131
Lucrece	82	King Lear	133
Romeo and Juliet	85	Macbeth	136
King Richard II.	87	Antony and Cleopatra	139
King John	89	Coriolanus	140
The Merchant of Venice	91	Timon of Athens	142
King Henry IV. Parts I. & II	96	Pericles	144
King Henry V.	99	Cymbeline	146
The Taming of the Shrew	101	The Tempest	148
The Merry Wives of Windsor	103	The Winter's Tale	151
Much Ado about Nothing	106	King Henry VIII.	153
As You Like It	108	Doubtful Plays	156
The Passionate Pilgrim	110		

CHAPTER VII.
SHAKSPERE FROM 1616 TO 1877 158

APPENDIX.
BOOKS USEFUL TO STUDENTS OF SHAKSPERE . . 166

N.B.—The references to Act, Scene, and Line, throughout, are to The Globe Shakespeare.

LITERATURE PRIMERS.

SHAKSPERE.

CHAPTER I.

THE ELIZABETHAN DRAMA.

1. **England in Shakspere's Youth.**—In the closing years of the sixteenth century the life of England ran high. The revival of learning had enriched the national mind with a store of new ideas and images; the reformation of religion had been accomplished, and its fruits were now secure; three conspiracies against the Queen's life had recently been foiled, and her rival, the Queen of Scots, had perished on the scaffold; the huge attempt of Spain against the independence of England had been defeated by the gallantry of English seamen, aided by the winds of heaven. English adventurers were exploring untravelled lands and distant oceans; English citizens were growing in wealth and importance; the farmers made the soil give up twice its former yield; the nobility, however fierce their private feuds and rivalries might be, gathered around the Queen as their centre. It was felt that England was a power in the continent of Europe. Men were in a temper to think human life, with its action and its passions, a very important and interesting thing. They did not turn away from this world, and

despise it in comparison with a heavenly country, as did many of the finest souls in the Middle Ages; they did not, like the writers of the age of Queen Anne, care only for "the town:" it was man they cared for, and the whole of manhood—its good and evil, its greatness and grotesqueness, its laughter and its tears.

When men cared thus about human life, their imagination craved living pictures and visions of it. They liked to represent to themselves men and women in all passionate and mirthful aspects and circumstances of life. Sculpture, which the Greeks so loved, would not have satisfied them, for it is too simple and too calm; music would not have been sufficient, for it is too purely an expression of feelings, and says too little about actions and events. The art which suited the temper of their imagination was the drama. In the drama they saw men and women, alive, in action, in suffering, changing for ever from mood to mood, from attitude to attitude; they saw these men and women solitary, conversing with their own hearts—in pairs and in groups, acting one upon another; in multitudes, swayed hither and thither by their leaders.

2. **Pre-Shaksperian Drama.**—The drama had been at first connected with the Church. It represented, both to instruct and to amuse the people, events of sacred history and of the lives of saints, or threw into the form of a play some moral allegory, enlivened by grotesque incidents. Out of this rude early drama had grown, by the time that Shakspere began to write, three or four divergent branches. (*a*) Allegorical plays—fashionable at Court—were still written; but the allegories instead of treating a theme from Christian morals were in general founded upon classical mythology, and were often meant as elaborate compliments to the Queen or some great nobles. (*b*) There were tragedies, and in some of these elements of real tragic grandeur existed; but they were

marred by much crudeness and extravagance, by a revelling in coarse horrors of mere violence and blood. (*c*) There were comedies, at times not without a portion of true grace and beauty, but often degenerating into vulgar buffoonery and the antics of a clown. (*d*) There were historical plays, in which some of the patriotic feeling of Englishmen, and their interest in our national annals, embodied themselves; but these too often spread out into a series of loosely connected scenes; they lacked unity of subject and coherence of form. Some of Shakspere's predecessors, or fellow-playwrights, who made their mark earlier than he, had given each some gift of his own to the drama, and helped to bring it forward to the point at which Shakspere took it up; but none of them was able to raise tragedy, comedy, and history out of their crudities and puerilities into truly great and noble forms of art. *John Lyly* had shown how a bright and lively dialogue can be written in prose. *George Peele* had produced dramatic verse of a sweet but monotonous melody. A romantic spirit was introduced into English comedy by *Robert Greene*; over his poetry breathes the fresh air of English meadows; his style is more free, more bright, light, and natural than that of any preceding dramatic poet. Above all, much was due to *Christopher Marlowe*. His genius was essentially of a tragic cast; from his veins the life-blood of passion had flowed into the drama of England, and forthwith it lost its timidity, and was conscious of strange new force and fire; in his tragedies was first heard upon a public stage that measure, which is the express voice in our poetry of dramatic feeling — blank verse. (See Mr. Brooke's Primer: *English Literature*, pp. 74–82.)

3. **Theatres and Actors.**—The companies of actors sought protection and patronage from the Queen, or from some great noble, and accordingly styled themselves by such names as "the Queen's servants," "the Earl of Leicester's servants," "the

Lord Chamberlain's servants." When a command was given they played at Court for a circle of aristocratic spectators. More frequently they played before a mixed audience of high and low in some inn-yard, or in one of the London theatres. Of these the first was built by *James Burbage* (father of the great actor *Richard Burbage*, who took the chief part in several of Shakspere's plays), in the year 1576. It was erected "in the fields," in the parish of Shoreditch, and was named "The Theatre." Almost at the same time, and in the same locality, rose a second theatre, known as "The Curtain," from the name of the piece of ground upon which it stood. While the Queen, the Court, and the pleasure-loving part of the populace favoured and supported the stage, it was looked on with hostility by devout Puritans, and by the civic authorities, the Lord Mayor and Corporation of London. The gathering of crowds led to occasional brawls, in which the London apprentices did not fail to display their prowess. Public morality, it was said, suffered through temptations offered by the place and the occasion. In times of plague, stricken persons and persons who had but partially recovered, carried infection with them to the theatres, and so spread the sickness. When moved thereto, the players dared to satirise eminent living persons upon the stage. On Sundays folk were enticed away from the congregation of saints to the devil's congregation at the playhouse. So argued the city authorities, and with them some sober-minded men and women of the Puritan way of thinking. As a consequence the players were glad to erect their theatres in some easily accessible place just beyond the boundary of the Lord Mayor's jurisdiction. To the theatre "in the fields" the common people could easily walk; gentlefolk could ride, and have their horses held by some theatrical underling at the door while the performance was taking place. To the theatres erected at a later time on the Bankside,

Southwark, gentlemen would go in one of the boats plied by the Thames watermen; the rest would choose the more circuitous route by London Bridge.

4. **Performance of a Play.**—Within the theatre a miscellaneous crowd assembled. Most commonly the performance began at three o'clock and lasted from two to three hours. In the public theatres the centre of the building was open to the sky and without seats, only the stage and the gallery being roofed, and admission to the open space, or "yard," cost from one penny or twopence to sixpence, while as much as a shilling, two shillings, or half-a-crown was given to obtain a place in the best parts of the house. The private theatres were fully roofed, and during a performance the interior was lit with torches. Upon the rush-strewn stage sat young gallants, who drank and smoked and joked while they waited for the appearance of the black-robed Prologue. Below, apprentices, tradesmen, sailors, and low women crushed and swayed, cracked nuts, and fought for bitten apples. If ladies appeared in the "rooms," or boxes, it was considered correct that they should conceal their faces behind masks. In due time a flourish of trumpets announced that the play was to begin, and a flag was hung out from the top of the building. Upon the trumpet's third sounding the prologue was delivered, the curtain divided and drew back, and the actors were discovered. They appeared in costumes which were often costly, but which made slight pretension to historical propriety. Of movable scenery there was none. The stage was hung with arras, and overhead a blue canopy represented "the heavens." Sometimes when a tragedy was to be enacted the stage-hangings were black. At the back of the stage was a balcony which served for many purposes—"it was inner room, upper room, window, balcony, battlements, hill-side, Mount Olympus, any place in fact which was supposed to be separated from and above the scene of the main action." Here Juliet appeared to Romeo,

and probably here the play-king and play-queen in *Hamlet* enacted their parts. A change of scene was indicated by some suggestive piece of stage furniture —a bed to signify a bed-chamber; a table with pens upon it to signify a counting-house; or, more simply, a board bearing in large letters the name of the place intended was brought upon the stage. Accordingly, the dramatist might change the scene as often as he pleased, or indulge in magnificent description, without fear that a lessee would offer as an objection the expense of providing suitable scenery. While the play was going forward the clown would amuse the audience with extempore joking, not set down by the poet. Shakspere disliked this traditional mode of providing sport for the occupants of the yard or pit—the "groundlings," as they were called—and his Hamlet, when delivering his advice to the players, warns them against such an abuse in their performance of the tragedy which he commands them to present. (Act III. Sc. ii. L. 42.) Between the acts there was dancing and singing, and at the end of the play the clown put the audience into good humour before they separated with a jig, that is, a farcical song accompanied by dancing and the music of his pipe or tabor. (See *Twelfth Night*, end.) Sometimes a short epilogue was delivered. (*As You Like It*, and *Tempest*, end.) Finally the actors knelt and offered up a prayer for the Queen. It is important to note that the female parts were played by boys or young men. The parts of Desdemona and Imogen, of Cleopatra and Lady Macbeth could not be entrusted to a great actress, as they have been since the Restoration, but were left to the mercy of some youth with unbroken voice. (See *Antony and Cleopatra*, Act V. Sc. ii. L. 220; *Hamlet*, Act II. Sc. ii. L. 444; *As You Like It*, Epilogue.) A further refinement of art was demanded from these young actors when they were required to represent a girl who has assumed the disguise of male attire, as happens with Shakspere's Viola, with Jessica and Portia, with Rosalind, with Imogen; it was necessary that they should at once pretend to be and avoid becoming that which they actually were.

5. **Writers of Plays sometimes Actors.**—In several instances, though not in all, the writers of plays were also actors. Thus they studied their public from the boards, acquired an instinctive feeling for what would hit the general taste, and for what would only perplex or offend, and gained a mastery over the secrets of stage effect. Certain qualities, it was found, were indispensable in a play which was intended to give immediate pleasure; and, on the other hand, many particulars which would have seemed to a writer in his closet of essential importance, were found to be matters of indifference in an acting play that aimed at success rather than scholarly or artistic exactitude. Attaining what was all-important, the poet was careless about much beside, and in some cases Shakspere does not scruple to use devices for producing a kind of stage-perspective of time and space which, if examined without reference to the purposes of stage effect, seem mere blunders, just as in some great painting a needful piece of colour, if not looked at from the right point of view, may appear an unintelligible blot. The movement and spectacle upon the stage is never despised by Shakspere. Even in *Hamlet*, which has rightly been named a "tragedy of thought," what an impressive series of appeals to the senses is made from first to last—the starlit night upon the platform at Elsinore, haunted by a majestic spirit from the grave, succeeded by the brilliancy of the Danish Court surrounding the sad, black-robed figure of Prince Hamlet, and so on, past that scene in which the crazed Ophelia appears singing her snatches of song and bestowing her flowers, to the close, where the murderers and the murdered man alike fall in death, and the "quarry cries on havock."

6. **Plays considered as Property.**—The writer of a play usually sold it to the theatre, but sometimes

to a kind of broker who stood between players and authors, buying from the one, and selling, so as himself to profit by the transaction, to the other. Such was *Philip Henslowe*, a dyer, pawnbroker, theatrical lessee and speculator, who during the years of Shakspere's authorship had many dramatic poets in his pay. His diary still exists, and from it we learn that the highest price given by him for a play before the year 1600 was £8; the lowest sum is £4; while for an embroidered velvet cloak no less than £16 is given, and £4 14s. for a pair of hose. After 1600 the price of a play rose to £20 if the dramatist was one of repute. Not infrequently the plays, for which such moderate prices were given, had been the work of two or more hands, a sudden demand for a new play inducing the company to set several authors to work, in order that time might be gained. Or the double authorship was the result of a more lasting alliance between two writers of kindred or complementary genius, who found that they could be helpful to one another in this way. Or, again, it arose from a later poet going over the work of some earlier dramatist and recasting his play, or adding to it certain scenes which might serve to give it the charm of at least partial novelty. The theatrical company having bought the manuscript of a play were naturally desirous to keep it for their own uses upon the stage, and were unwilling that it should pass into the hands of a bookseller, and be published. But the lovers of the drama liked to be able to buy and read a popular play; and accordingly piratical publishers tried in some dishonest way to come at the manuscript. When that was impossible they sent reporters to the playhouse, who copied down the words as they fell from the actors' lips, but sometimes so imperfectly that gaps in the reporters' copies had to be supplied by some mercenary scribbler, who generally succeeded in spoiling not only the sound but the sense of such passages as he attempted to handle. Such an imperfect report of *Hamlet*, in an earlier form of the play than that which it finally assumed, we possess, with passages stupidly inserted by an unknown hand, or reproduced from an imperfect recollection of what Shakspere had written.

CHAPTER II.

THE LIFE OF SHAKSPERE.

7. Stratford. Birth of Shakspere.—Warwickshire has been named by Shakspere's contemporary and fellow-poet, Michael Drayton, "the heart of England." The country around Stratford presents the perfection of quiet English scenery; it is remarkable for its wealth of lovely wild-flowers, for its deep meadows on each side of the tranquil Avon, and for its rich, sweet woodlands. The town itself, in Shakspere's time, numbered about 1400 inhabitants; a town of scattered timber houses, possessing two chief buildings—the stately church by the river-side, and the Guildhall, where companies of players would at times perform, when the corporation secured their services. Flood and fire were the chief dangers of the town. The quiet river often rose angrily in autumn, and left disease behind it. The plague, in its course, did not turn aside from Stratford. Here, and probably in a low-ceiled room of a house in Henley Street, William Shakspere was born, in April, 1564. Upon what day we cannot be certain; but upon the 26th he was baptised; and there is a tradition that the day of his death was the anniversary of his birthday. Allowing for the difference between old style and new, April 23rd corresponds with our 3rd of May, or, allowing for the accumulated error in the new style, with our May 5th.

8. Shakspere's Parentage.—*John Shakspere*, father of the future dramatist, was a prosperous burgess of Stratford. He made and sold gloves, farmed land, and though he knew not how to write his name, became an important public person of the town, tasting ale for his fellow-burgesses, keeping the Queen's peace, imposing fines upon offenders, rising in course of time to the honourable posts of chamberlain, alderman, and high bailiff. He married, in 1557, *Mary Arden*, daughter of his landlord, who had died about a year before, leaving Mary a considerable piece of landed property in possession (including a farm at Ashbies), and one much more valuable in reversion. The Ardens were Warwickshire gentry since before the Conquest, and two of the family had held places of distinction in the household of Henry VII. The first child and the second of John and Mary Shakspere were girls, who died while infants; the third— their first-born son—was to live, in spite of the plague which desolated Stratford during the year of his birth, and was to write the plays and poems that we know. Other children followed: a daughter, who survived William Shakspere, and is remembered in his will; another daughter, who died early; and three sons— Gilbert, who is said to have lived until the Restoration, and to have talked as an old man of his great brother's impersonation of Adam in *As You Like It* (but this is doubtful); Richard; and Edmund, who became an actor, and died in London in the year 1607.

9. **Schooling and Recreations.**—To the Free Grammar School of Stratford William Shakspere was sent, we may be sure, to learn what neither his father nor his mother could teach. There he was taught not only English, but some Latin, and perhaps a little Greek. The amount of Shakspere's classical learning has been described by his more scholarly fellow-playwright, Ben Jonson, as "small Latin and less Greek;" and it is certain that, in using Greek and Latin authors for the purposes of his plays, he went to translations rather than to the originals. But that he had got by heart his *Lily's Latin Grammar*,

and was acquainted with the rudiments of that language is almost certain; and it has been noticed that he uses several English words—as, for example, the *continents* of rivers for containing banks, *quantity* for value, and others—in senses which would not occur to one who was absolutely ignorant of Latin. Afterwards—perhaps during his London life—Shakspere seems to have learned something of French, and possibly also of Italian.

In the first year in which Shakspere could have been admitted to the Free Grammar School, his father became chief alderman of Stratford. The corporation seem to have welcomed the players who occasionally visited the town. Now and again sums of money are paid by the chamberlain to "the Earl of Leicester's players," "my Lord of Warwick's players," and "the Earl of Worcester's players." The boy, his father's eldest son, may have been taken to see the entertainments in the Guildhall. Coventry is not very far distant from Stratford; and it is not impossible that Shakspere, as a boy or youth, may have watched the guilds set up the pageants in the streets of that ancient city at the festival of Corpus Christi; may have observed Herod with his painted mask and violent bearing (*Hamlet*, Act III. Sc. ii. L. 16), and the "black souls"—the souls of the damned—in their garb of black and yellow stripes, to whom, in *Henry V.* (Act II. Sc. iii. L. 42-44), the flea upon Bardolph's fiery nose is compared. In the summer of 1575 Queen Elizabeth made her famous visit to Kenilworth, and was entertained by Leicester with splendid and varied ceremonies and spectacles. From Stratford it is only a few hours' walk to Kenilworth; Shakspere's father might ride across with the boy before him. And a celebrated passage in *A Midsummer Night's Dream* (Act II. Sc. i. L. 148-168), where Oberon describes to Puck some marvels he had seen, so accurately depicts some of the Kenilworth shows on this occasion that we can well believe that

Shakspere here does not invent, but rather recalls what his eyes had actually looked on. (See p. 74.)

10. **His Father's Decline in Fortune.**—Until about Shakspere's thirteenth or fourteenth year, his father seems to have been a prosperous man. But from 1578 onwards for a number of years, the fortunes of John Shakspere declined. To raise money he mortgages the farm at Ashbies; he is not required to pay the weekly levy for relief of the poor; borough taxes levied upon him in 1579 are entered as "unpaid and unaccounted for;" he is in debt to one Roger Sadler; he sells his wife's share, and soon afterwards her reversionary interest in the Snitterfield property. Six years later we find his case grown worse: upon a distraint issued against him—a writ to seize his goods for debt—the return is made that John Shakspere has nothing in which he is able to be distrained; he is deprived of his alderman's office on the ground that he "doth not come to the hall, nor hath not done of long time." Is he afraid of arrest? In the following year, 1587, it would seem that he actually was arrested, for we find him suing out a writ of *habeas corpus*. So late as 1592, when a commission was appointed to inquire into the conformity of the Warwickshire people to the established religion, John Shakspere's failure to appear monthly at church is set down as caused by the fear of "processe for debt." Still he seems to have clung to some fragments of his property, and to have retained some of the old esteem of his fellow-citizens. At this period his son was beginning to be known as a successful dramatist; and it is almost certain that, owing to William Shakspere's energy and affection, the old man was restored to a position of comfort, which he enjoyed until his death in 1601.

In consequence of his father's difficulties, it is likely that William Shakspere was withdrawn from school, and either assisted John Shakspere in his trade, or was set to earn a living in some way for himself. What his precise employment was, in the interval between leaving school and leaving Stratford, is a question which affords room for much guessing, but one which cannot be answered with certainty. One tradition says that he was "bound apprentice to a butcher;" another, that he was "a schoolmaster in the country;" while certain supposed references to him by the dramatist *Nash*, together with the number and accuracy of the legal allusions in his writings, have led many persons to believe that he was for a time at work in an attorney's office. But it is doubtful whether *Nash's* description of "a sort of shifting companions that run through every art and thrive by none," who "leave the trade of *Noverint* [that is the legal profession], whereto they were born, and busy themselves with the endeavours of art"—it is doubtful whether these words of *Nash* have any reference to Shakspere; and, in the course of his father's many law-suits, a clever youth could hardly have failed to gain some acquaintance with legal terms and procedures.

11. **Shakspere's Marriage.**—What we know for certain is that in his nineteenth year Shakspere was making grave engagements and accepting serious duties. In November, 1582, the Bishop of Worcester granted a licence for the marriage of William Shakspere and *Anne Hathaway* upon once asking of the banns. Their first child, Susanna, was baptised May 26th, 1583. Anne was the daughter of Richard Hathaway, a substantial yeoman, living at Shottery, a beautiful hamlet hardly one mile distant from Stratford. She was eight years older than her boy husband. The friends of the bride (her father had been five months dead) seem to have desired the marriage, and perhaps urged it on, that Anne's child might be born in lawful wedlock. Whether it proved a happy marriage or the reverse—so little do we know of Shakspere's life—remains a matter of mere conjecture. For four or five years he resided in Stratford, and in 1585 became the father of twins, Hamnet and Judith,

named after his friends Hamnet Sadler and his wife. Most probably during the poet's London life Anne with his children stayed in Stratford. It was in Stratford, in 1596, that Hamnet, his only son, was buried. But though Shakspere chose to leave his wife and children in the country, while he himself was toiling in the great city, a tradition records that he paid a yearly visit to his home; there is no doubt that he toiled with the purpose of returning—as he actually did—to his native town, there, with his wife and daughters about him, to spend the later years of his life. In Shakspere's will the only mention of his wife occurs in an interlineation, by which is bequeathed to her "my second best bed with the furniture;" she was, however, legally provided for, having as widow the right of dower in Shakspere's freehold property. The bequest of a bed was surely not meant as a parting insult from her husband; we must rather understand it as meant to gratify some womanly attachment to a piece of household goods, founded, it may be, on old and tender associations. From the poet's writings no certain inference can be drawn with regard to his marriage. In *A Midsummer Night's Dream* (Act I. Sc. i. L. 137) mention is made of love "misgraffed in respect of years," as a cause of trouble in love's course; and in *Twelfth Night* (Act II. Sc. iv. L. 30-40) may be found a much more noteworthy passage, in which the Duke speaks to Viola about the risk a woman older than her husband runs of losing his affection. Such evidence as Shakspere's *Sonnets* afford points in the same direction. On the other hand, there is no bitterness, open or covert, against women in general, or any particular type or class of women in Shakspere's writings. Even the shrewish women of some of his early plays, introduced for comic purposes, are at heart loving and loyal, like Adriana of *The Comedy of Errors*; or only outrageously spoilt children, but not incapable of being reclaimed, like Katharina in *The Taming of the Shrew*. It is observable, however, that all through his plays Shakspere shows a peculiar comprehension of the situation of a woman who, throwing aside conventional but not real modesty, ventures upon certain greater or less advances towards the man she loves. From Juliet to Miranda, a series of Shaksperian heroines could be named, who share, as it were, in their own wooing, without once forfeiting their ardent purity of soul. Upon the whole it seems probable that, while the union of Shakspere and his wife was not one of the rare, flawless, married unions, yet it was founded at first upon strong mutual attraction; and that, if a period of estrangement, slight or serious, intervened, there was found on both sides substantial worth enough to make it natural that their lives should come really together again, and that it should be indeed good for each to accept things as they were.

12. **Deer-Stealing. Leaves Stratford.**—The immediate cause of Shakspere's departure from Stratford is thus told circumstantially by *Rowe*, his first biographer: "He had, by a misfortune common enough to young fellows, fallen into ill company; and, amongst them, some that made a frequent practice of deer-stealing, engaged him, more than once, in robbing a park that belonged to *Sir Thomas Lucy*, of Charlcote, near Stratford. For this he was prosecuted by that gentleman, as he thought, somewhat too severely; and in order to revenge the ill-usage, he made a ballad upon him. And though this, probably the first, essay of his poetry be lost, yet it is said to have been so very bitter, that it redoubled the prosecution against him, to that degree, that he was obliged to leave his business and family in Warwickshire for some time, and shelter himself in London." Some of the details of this story are undoubtedly incorrect, but there is good reason to believe that a foundation of truth underlies the tradition. *Sir T. Lucy* was an important person in the neighbourhood—a member of Parliament, one of the Puritan party (with which our dramatist can never

have been in sympathy), and about the time of this alleged deer-stealing frolic, was concerned in framing a bill in Parliament for the preservation of game. Although he did not possess what is properly a park at Charlcote, he had deer; Shakspere and his companions may have had a struggle with *Sir T. Lucy's* men. A verse of the ballad ascribed to the young poacher has been traditionally handed down, and in it the writer puns upon the name Lucy—"O lowsie Lucy"—in a way sufficiently insulting. It is noteworthy that in the first scene of *The Merry Wives of Windsor*, Justice Shallow is introduced as highly incensed against Sir John Falstaff, who has beaten his men, killed his deer, and broke open his lodge; the Shallows, like Shakspere's old antagonist, have "luces" in their coat-of-arms, and the Welsh parson admirably misunderstands the word—"the dozen white louses do become an old coat well." It can hardly be doubted that when this scene was written, Shakspere had some grudge against the Lucy family, and in making them ridiculous before the Queen he may have had an amused sense that he was now obtaining a success for his boyish lampoon, little dreamed of when it was originally put into circulation among the good folk of Stratford.

13. **Early Years in London. Greene's Allusion.**—From the baptism of his twins, in February, 1584-85, we hear nothing of Shakspere (except the mention of his name in an action in the Queen's Bench, brought by his father against John Lambert, who now held the Ashbies property), until he is spoken of in 1592 as a successful actor and author. The "Queen's Players" came to Stratford in 1587. Then perhaps it was that Shakspere decided to leave his native town, and seek his fortune in the world of London. A story, alleged to have come from *Sir W. Davenant*, that Shakspere's first employment in connection with the theatre, was that of holding the horses of those who came to the play, we may dismiss as probably mythical. It has

been maintained that a passage in Spenser's *Tears of the Muses* (1590-91), where the Muse of Comedy laments that

> Our pleasant *Willy*, ah! is dead of late,

refers to some temporary cessation of Shakspere from dramatic authorship; but the probability is that someone else is meant, perhaps John Lyly, perhaps the comic actor, Tarleton, who had but lately died when Spenser wrote the poem. The first certain reference to Shakspere which has been discovered is that of the dramatist *Robert Greene* in his *Greenes Groatsworth of Wit bought with a Million of Repentance*, a pamphlet written by its unhappy author upon his deathbed, and published immediately after Greene's death by his executor, *Henry Chettle*. Here the dying playwright, addressing three of his fellow-authors, who have been identified with Marlowe, Peele, and Nash (or Lodge), warns them against putting any trust in players: "Yes, trust them not: for there is an upstart Crow, beautified with our feathers, that with his *tygers heart wrapt in a players hide*, supposes he is as well able to bumbast out a blanke verse as the best of you: and being an absolute *Johannes factotum*, is in his owne conceit the onely Shake-scene in a country." We have evidence here that before Greene's death the players had been turning from him to a rival poet who was also an actor, who could write a swelling blank verse like Marlowe, who turned his hand to everything, and made himself useful in many ways to his company. Him Greene hated, and he hoped that Marlowe and Nash might hate him also. The words "beautified with our feathers," probably mean no more than pranking himself as an actor in the fine speeches of our plays, but the words "tygers heart wrapped in a players hide" parody a line—

> Oh tygers heart wrapt in a woman's hide—

which occurs in the *True Tragedie of Richard, Duke of*

York, and is also found in the *Third Part of Henry VI.*, this last being a recast, with additions and omissions, of the *True Tragedie*. It has been suggested that in quoting this line Greene reminds his friends that Shakspere, in the *Third Part of Henry VI.*, had stolen from an earlier play of which Greene himself, or Marlowe, or both together were authors, and that therefore for them a peculiar ground of resentment against Shakspere existed.

14. **Chettle's Reference to Shakspere.**—Some three months later, in December, 1592, a pamphlet by *Henry Chettle* appeared, entitled *Kind-Harts Dream*. It seems that Marlowe and Shakspere took offence at passages in *Greenes Groatsworth* referring to them. Chettle declares that as for one of them (Marlowe), while he reverences his learning he has nothing to answer for, and cares not ever to make his acquaintance. To Shakspere he offers a liberal apology. "The other [Shakspere] whome at that time I did not so much spare as since I wish I had . . . . . I am as sory as if the originall fault had beene my fault, because my selfe have seene his demeanor no lesse civill, than he exelent in the qualitie he professes; besides, divers of worship have reported his uprightnes of dealing, which argues his honesty, and his facetious grace in writting, that aprooves his art." The word "quality," it should be noted, was used in Shakspere's time with special reference to the actor's profession ; so that we here possess testimony to Shakspere's worth as a man, to his excellence in his profession, and to the friends and fame he had already acquired as a writer.* If the poet whom *Spenser* speaks of in his *Colin Clout's Come Home Again*, under the name of Ætion be Shakspere—and though *Colin Clout* was not published until 1594, there are reasons for thinking that it may have been written as early as 1591—it is interesting to see the "upstart crow" of the envious

---

* "Facetious," in the quotation from Chettle, means felicitous, or happy.

Greene recognised, by one so much greater than Greene, as a young eagle in boldness and strength of flight (Aëtion = Ἀετίων from ἀετός, an eagle).

> And there though last not least is Aetion:
> A gentler shepherd may no where be found;
> Whose muse, full of high thought's invention,
> Doth like himself heroically sound.

"Like himself," that is, like his name *Shake-speare*; but the reference may be to Drayton, who had written under the heroic name of *Rowland*.

15. **Southampton and Shakspere.**—To the young *Earl of Southampton*, nine years junior to himself—probably one of those persons of worship who had come forward to vindicate Shakspere from Greene's aspersions—the poet dedicated, in 1593, *Venus and Adonis*, "the first heire of my invention." It proved a distinguished literary success, and in the following year, 1594, the *Lucrece* appeared, with a dedication to the same noble person, written, not in terms of timid appeal, like the earlier dedication, but in words of strong and confident affection. "What I have done is yours; what I have to do is yours; being part of all I have, devoted yours." The Earl, a generous and high-spirited youth, like those young men who make bright the early comedies of Shakspere, had no doubt warmly recognised Shakspere's genius. There is a story, professing to have come from Davenant, which represents Southampton as having at one time given to Shakspere £1000 to go through with a purchase he had a mind to. This is doubtless an exaggeration; but that Southampton was at this time a warm and generous friend we may not doubt, and Shakspere, the scapegrace of his native town, scoffed at by Greene, one of the despised players, bound to a way of life utterly distasteful to him, responded warmly, and gave up his heart in unrestrained delight, to one who seemed so noble and so liberal of love.

16. **Growing Prosperity.**—*Ben Jonson*, in his lines to the memory of Shakspere, addressing him as "Sweet swan of Avon," speaks of

> Those flights upon the banks of Thames
> That so did take Eliza and our James!

The first mention we possess of Shakspere by name, after his arrival in London, occurs in the accounts of the Treasurer of the Chamber, from which we learn that he appeared twice with Burbage, as a member of the Lord Chamberlain's company, before Queen Elizabeth, in Christmas time, 1593. He was now rapidly producing his historical plays and earlier comedies, and was gathering that wealth which he meant should release him from the servitude of his profession. He had planned to return in due time to Stratford, and to live there as a gentleman. In 1596 John Shakspere applied for a grant of coat-armour, and in the following year the grant was made by the Garter King-of-Arms. But if Shakspere hoped to found a family that hope received a blow, and the father's heart was wounded by the death, in 1596, of Hamnet, his only son. Still, however, he pursues his plan, and looks forward to Stratford as his home. An attempt was made at this time by John Shakspere and his wife to recover the ancestral fields of Ashbies, probably without success. In the same year, 1597, William Shakspere bought, for £60, New Place, a goodly dwelling in his native town. His interest in his country home and his influence in London are recognised in a letter of 1598, still existing, from Master Abraham Sturley to Richard Quiney (father of Shakspere's future son-in-law). Quiney was in London, soliciting Lord Burleigh for certain favours to be conferred on the town of Stratford; Sturley supposes that by the friends Mr. Shakspere can make their mark may be hit. Later in the year was written by Quiney the only letter addressed to our great poet which remains to us; its purport is the practical one of begging a loan of £30; we may surmise that Shakspere acceded to his friend's request. He has property in both Stratford and London; in the former we find him a considerable holder of corn and malt; in the latter he is assessed on property in the parish of St. Helen's, Bishopsgate, £5 13s. 4d.

17. **Growing Fame. Meres.**—But we have not yet exhausted the information which this year 1598 yields. Now it is that Ben Jonson's first comedy, *Every Man in his Humour*, makes its appearance. There is a tradition that the play was brought before the public through the good offices of Shakspere; it is certain that he acted in the play, taking, probably, the part of Knowell. Now, also (1598), most remarkable testimony to the high position occupied by Shakspere as a dramatist and as a narrative and lyrical poet is given in the *Palladis Tamia, Wit's Treasury*, by Francis Meres, Master of Arts. The passage in which Meres enumerates twelve of Shakspere's plays is of the utmost importance in guiding us towards a true chronology of his works, and will afterwards be quoted at length; it must also be observed that Meres makes mention of Shakspere's "sugred sonnets among his private friends." The earliest editions of plays by Shakspere belong to this period. In 1597 were printed *Richard II.*, *Richard III.*, and *Romeo and Juliet*. Others speedily followed. It is clear that in several instances the copies were obtained surreptitiously, and to gain a sale for plays by other authors unscrupulous printers now placed the popular name of Shakspere upon the title page. In 1599 a volume of poems, entitled *The Passionate Pilgrim*, was published, and its authorship ascribed to Shakspere: Jaggard, the publisher, had got hold of a few short pieces of Shakspere's, and added to these liberally from other quarters. We know, on the testimony of *Heywood*, that Shakspere, upon occasion of a subsequent edition containing poems falsely ascribed to him, was seriously offended.

18. **Practical Energy.**—In 1601 died at Stratford John Shakspere. Still his son worked on to win for himself independence and a home. *Hamlet* is entered in Stationers' register, 1602, and in the same year the creator of *Hamlet*, a shareholder in the Globe Theatre since 1599, was living in no dream-world, but was taking practical possession of this solid earth—purchasing in May, for £320, one hundred and seven acres in the parish of Old Stratford, his brother Gilbert receiving the conveyance for him—and later in the year (the author of *Hamlet* being now "William Shakspere, *Gentleman*") a second and smaller property. His largest purchase was that of the unexpired term of a lease of the tithes of Stratford, Old Stratford, Bishopton, and Welcombe; this he acquired in July, 1605, for the sum of £440. A year previously, when perhaps he was writing his *King Lear*, his care for practical affairs appears by his bringing an action, in the court of Stratford, against one Philip Rogers, for £1 15s. 10d., being the price of malt sold and delivered to him at different times. Shakspere seems to have found it possible to carry on actively and at the same time his life in the ideal, and his life in the material world.

19. **Family Joys and Sorrows.**—But although now styled "gentleman, of Stratford-on-Avon," he had not yet left London nor abandoned his profession. Elizabeth died in 1603; it was noticed at the time (by *Chettle*, who refers to his great contemporary under the title of "silver-tongued *Melicert*") that Shakspere lamented the Queen in no ode or elegy. In May arrived at London her successor, James I., and within a few days after his arrival a warrant was issued licensing the theatrical company to which Shakspere belonged; his name appears second in the list of players contained in the warrant. Ben Jonson's *Sejanus* was first acted in the same year, 1603, and the name of Shakspere occupies a place in the list of actors. We know that Burbage on pur-

chasing the lease of Blackfriars (1603) placed players there among whom was Shakspere; at what time he ceased to appear upon the stage we cannot say. Nor do we know when, precisely, he returned to Stratford. In 1607 happiness and sorrow came to him: on June 5, his eldest and favourite daughter, *Susanna*, aged twenty-four, was married to *Mr. John Hall*, a practising physician of considerable repute; then, doubtless, the poet was with his daughter on her wedding-day. On the last day of the year his youngest brother, *Edmund*, was buried in the church of St. Saviour's, Southwark. *Edmund*, was a player attracted, perhaps, to London by his brother's success; his age was twenty-seven. William Shakspere did not apparently despise the ceremonial part of life, for we find that on this occasion twenty shillings were paid for "a forenoon knell of the great bell." Again, within a few months, death visited his household; in September, 1608, *Mary Shakspere*, who had lived to see her son so famous and wealthy, followed her husband to the grave. It is not improbable that Shakspere may have been present at her deathbed, for a month later he was at Stratford, and stood sponsor for William Walker, who is remembered in his will. His mother had not died without having held in her arms a grandchild of her son. On February 21, 1607–8 was baptised a daughter of John and Susanna Hall, whom they named Elizabeth; she was their only child, and the only one of his grandchildren whom Shakspere lived to see.

20. **Return to Stratford.**—Between the years 1610 and 1612 we have reason to suppose that Shakspere returned for good to his Stratford home. The change was great from the streets of London, the noisy theatres, the brilliant wit-combats at the Mermaid tavern, to the peaceful retreat, the wife whom he had loved as a boy—now grown elderly—his children and their little girl, by this time running about and talking, and, encircling these, the

quiet fields and hills and brimming river. Still he retained an interest in London. The Globe Theatre was perhaps yielding him some of the profits upon which he lived, and in March, 1613, he bought a house near Blackfriars Theatre, and leased it to a tenant for ten years. The death of *Richard Shakspere* in 1612 left him brotherless, unless *Gilbert* still survived. In the following year, 1613, the Globe Theatre was destroyed by fire, and probably manuscripts of Shakspere's plays perished on that occasion. Fire again may have alarmed, if it did not injure, Shakspere in 1614, for in that year a great conflagration took place at Stratford, fifty-four houses being burnt down. At the same time a project was put forward for the enclosing of some common lands near Stratford. It touched Shakspere's interests and would have been an injury to the poor: Shakspere resisted the scheme, declaring that "he was not able to bear the enclosing of Welcombe." We must not fail to notice one entry of the year 1614 in the Stratford Chamberlain's accounts: "Item: For one quart of sack, and one quart of clarett wine, given to a preacher at the *Newe Place*, xxd." Stratford had been growing puritanical since the time when Shakspere was a boy, and the players so often visited the town; at last the players were even paid *not* to perform. Mrs. Hall and her husband did not forfeit the poet's regard because they were somewhat puritanically inclined. Perhaps Shakspere's wife had sought in religion a satisfaction which her marriage had not afforded. We can imagine the great interpreter of life listening with a grave smile to the whole truth as proclaimed by the preacher, and recognising as a pleasant foible the preacher's interest in claret and sherry sack.

21. **Death.**—On February 10th, 1616, Shakspere's younger daughter, *Judith*, now aged 31, was married to *Thomas Quincy*, a vintner of Stratford, whose father —a friend of the poet—had been high bailiff of the town. On the 25th of the next month he executed

his will, which in January had been drawn, and in another month the world had lost Shakspere. He died April 23rd, 1616. Ward, the Vicar of Stratford, noted some fifty years later, "Shakespeare, Drayton, and Ben Jonson had a merry meeting, and, it seems, drank too hard, for Shakespeare died of a fever there contracted." Whether this be history or myth we cannot assert. In his will, while the main bulk of his property is left to Susanna Hall and her husband, his daughter Judith, his sister Joan, his godson, his Stratford friends, and some of his fellow-players are carefully remembered. Some months after the poet's death a son was born to Judith Quiney, whom she named Shakspere; but he died in his infancy, and neither of her other sons survived to middle life. The last living descendant of Shakspere was his granddaughter, Elizabeth Hall, who married a Mr. Nash, and, as his wife, entertained for three weeks, at New Place, Queen Henrietta Maria; and upon his decease married Mr. John Barnard, knighted by Charles II. in 1661.

22. **Portraits.**—Shakspere was buried in the parish church at Stratford. Within a few years after his death a bust of the poet was erected in the church. The face was probably modelled from a cast taken after death. It was originally coloured, and has been correctly re-coloured—the eyes hazel, the hair and beard auburn. This and the portrait engraved by *Droeshout*, which is prefixed to the First Folio, 1623, are the only certain likenesses of Shakspere which remain to us. But that known as the *Chandos* portrait, though differing in some important particulars from the other portraits, has by many persons been considered genuine; and there exists a death-mask—named, from a supposed former owner, the *Kesselstadt* death-mask—which bears the date 1616, and which *may* be the original cast from the dead poet's face. It exhibits a head of remarkable proportions, and a face of great power and refinement. The grave in the parish church at Stratford is

covered by a flat stone, bearing an inscription attributed to Shakspere himself.

> Good frend, for Jesus sake forbeare
> To digg the dust enclosed heare:
> Bleste be the man that spares thes stones,
> And curst be he that moves my bones.

CHAPTER III.

EARLY EDITIONS OF SHAKSPERE'S WRITINGS.

23. **Folios.**—The first collected edition of Shakspere's plays was the "Folio of 1623," set forth by his "friends" and "fellows" *John Heminge* and *Henry Condell*. It contains all the dramatic works usually found in modern editions (*e.g. The Globe Shakespeare*) except *Pericles*. The First Folio is dedicated to the Earls of Pembroke and of Montgomery. The editors speak depreciatingly of earlier "stolne and surreptitious copies;" and the sentence, "we have scarse received from him a blot in his papers," is meant to imply that they followed Shakspere's manuscript. Several of the plays in the Folio are however, in fact, printed from earlier quartos; while, in other cases, the quartos give a text superior to that of the Folio. Still the First Folio is of inestimable value, being, in some instances, more correct than the quartos, and containing eighteen plays of which no quarto editions exist.

"The Second Folio," 1632, is a reprint of the first, conjecturally emended to some extent, the emendations being more often wrong than right.

"The Third Folio," 1663 and 1664; the issue of 1664 contains seven additional plays, *viz. Pericles, Prince of Tyre; The London Prodigal; the History of the Life and Death of Thomas Lord Cromwell; The History of Sir John Oldcastle, the good Lord Cobham; The Puritan Widow; A Yorkshire Tragedy;* and *The Tragedy of Locrine*. Except a part of *Pericles*, it is almost certain that none of these plays are by Shakspere.

"The Fourth Folio" was printed in 1685.

24. **Quartos.**—But during Shakspere's lifetime, and throughout a large part of the 17th century, single plays of Shakspere appeared in quarto form ; some, no doubt, printed from Shakspere's manuscripts. The following table sets forth the most important facts about the quartos, the dates of the first editions (omitting all subsequent to 1630), &c. It will be seen that the largest number of quartos appeared in 1600 ; after that year measures must have been taken to prevent publication, nearly all the quartos of later date being such stolen or surreptitious copies as the editors of the First Folio condemn. Shakspere's name first appears on a quarto play, in 1598 (on *Love's Labour's Lost*), and after that date it is seldom absent from a title-page. In the following table * Q 1 means that the play was printed in the First Folio from the first Quarto edition ; * Q 2, from the second Quarto, and so on.

1593. *Venus and Adonis* (before the end of 1630 eleven quarto editions had appeared).
1594. (?) An edition of *Titus Andronicus*, not now extant.
,, *Lucrece* (before the end of 1624, six quartos).
1597. *Romeo and Juliet* (imperfect, pirated copy).
,, *Richard II.* (before the end of 1615, four quartos). * Q 5.
,, *Richard III.* (before the end of 1629, seven quartos, see p. 80).
1598. 1 *Henry IV.* (before the end of 1622, six quartos). * Q 5.
,, *Love's Labour's Lost* (with Shakspere's name for the first time on a play). * Q 1.
1599. *Passionate Pilgrim* (third edition in 1612 ; but only two now extant).
,, *Romeo and Juliet* (perfect, republished in 1609 ; and again, undated). * Q 3.
1600. 2 *Henry IV.*
,, *Midsummer Night's Dream* (two quartos in 1600, published (1) by Fishers (2) by Roberts). * Q 2.
,, *Merchant of Venice* (two quartos in 1600 (1) Roberts (2) Heyes). * Q 2.
,, *Much Ado about Nothing.* * Q 1.
,, *Titus Andronicus* (again in 1611). * Q 2.
,, *Henry V.* (imperfect, pirated copy ; before end of 1608 three quartos of imperfect *Henry V.*).
[Shakspere's name on all those of 1600, except *Titus Andronicus* and *Henry V.*]

1602. *Merry Wives of Windsor* (imperfect report of early form of the play; second quarto, 1619; with Shakspere's name).
1603. *Hamlet* (imperfect report of first form of the play; with Shakspere's name).
1604. *Hamlet* (later form; before the end of 1611, three quarto editions; with Shakspere's name).
1608. *Lear* (two quartos in 1608, surreptitious (?); with Shakspere's name).
1609. *Sonnets.*
,, *Troilus and Cressida* (two quartos in 1609, see p. 127; with Shakspere's name).
,, *Pericles* (before the end of 1630, five quartos; with Shakspere's name).
1622. *Othello* (second quarto, with alterations and corrections, in 1630).

CHAPTER IV.

EVIDENCE OF THE CHRONOLOGY OF SHAKSPERE'S WRITINGS.

25. **Chronological Method.**—The most fruitful method of studying the works of Shakspere is that which views them in the chronological order of their production. We thus learn something about their origin, their connection one with another, and their relation to the mind of their creator, as that mind passed from its early promise to its rich maturity and fulfilment. If we knew nothing about their date, we might well wonder how the same man could be the author of *Love's Labour's Lost* and of *King Lear*. Viewed in the chronological order we perceive that the one was the work of Shakspere's clever 'prentice hand, the other the outcome of his manhood with its sorrow and experience; and we can trace some portions at least of the path of transition from the earlier play to the later.

26. **Evidence of Chronology.**—The evidence which helps to ascertain the chronology of Shak-

spere's writings is of various kinds : I. Wholly external. II. Partly external and partly internal. III. Wholly internal.

I. **Wholly External.** (1) The publication of the poems and plays, and entries (either prior to or on publication) in the registers of the Stationers' Company. The play or poem may, of course, have been written long before it was published or entered on the Stationers' register; and on the other hand, entries in the register were sometimes made while a book was in contemplation or in hand, and before it was actually written. Setting aside the poems, *Venus and Adonis* (entered 1592), and *Lucrece* (1594), the earliest entry upon the register of an undoubted play by Shakspere is that of *King Richard II.* (August 29, 1597). The last plays to appear in a quarto edition during the poet's lifetime—I mean in a first quarto edition— were *Troilus and Cressida* and *Pericles* (1609).

(2) Mention of Shakspere's writings in contemporary books or documents of ascertained date. Thus *Manningham*, a student of the Middle Temple, notes in his Diary, Feb. 2, 1601-2, "At our feast wee had a play called *Twelve Night, or What You Will;*" and he goes on to describe Shakspere's comedy. In another Diary, that of *Dr. Simon Forman*, we find that, on April 20, 1610, he saw, for the first time, *Macbeth*, of the plot of which he makes a careful summary; again, on May 15, 1611, he saw at the Globe, *The Winter's Tale*, and again is at pains to set down the outlines of the story. The burning of the Globe Theatre, in June, 1613, during a performance of *King Henry VIII.*, is recorded by three witnesses. But to this class of evidence no single contribution is of equal importance with that of the list of plays given by *Meres*, in his *Palladis Tamia, Wits Treasury*, 1598: "As *Plautus* and *Seneca* are accounted the best for Comedy and Tragedy among the Latines, so Shakespeare among the English is the most excellent in both kinds for the stage: for Comedy,

witness his *Gentlemen of Verona*, his *Errors*, his *Love labors lost*, his *Love labours wonne*, his *Midsummers night dreame*, and his *Merchant of Venice*; for Tragedy, his *Richard the* 2, *Richard the* 3, *Henry the* 4, *King John*, *Titus Andronicus*, and his *Romeo and Juliet*." It will be noticed that Meres mentions six plays of each kind, preserving a balanced symmetry which he affects. Possibly he made omissions, possibly he pressed into his list the doubtful *Titus*, with the object of equalising the number of tragedies and comedies named by him. The *Love's Labour's Won* of Meres's list is generally believed to have been an earlier form of *All's Well that Ends Well*; but some critics have attempted to identify it with *The Taming of the Shrew*, some with *Much Ado*.

(3) Without express mention of a play of Shakspere, it may be clearly alluded to, or a quotation be made from it, or some passage may be imitated by a contemporary poet in a work the date of which is known. In some cases it is naturally difficult to decide whether Shakspere be the original owner of the thought or expression, or whether he himself be not the borrower; and there is the danger to be guarded against of imagining a connection between two passages which are really independent. It should be remembered also that, in the Elizabethan period, writings had often extensive circulation in manuscript before they were published. Guarding against these risks of error, this class of evidence is, however, of considerable importance. When, in Ben Jonson's *Every Man Out of His Humour*, 1599, we find mention of "Justice Silence," we cannot doubt that the second part of Shakspere's *Henry IV.* had been already upon the stage. In Weever's *Mirror of Martyrs*, 1601, occur the lines:

> The many-headed multitude were drawne
> By Brutus' speech, that Cæsar was ambitious;
> When eloquent Mark Antonie had showne
> His vertues, who but Brutus then was vicious?

We know of nothing which can have suggested these lines to Weever, except Shakspere's *Julius Cæsar*; in Plutarch no such scene exists. Some of the evidence under this head, although derived from sources outside the works of Shakspere, yet implies an acquaintance with passages in those works, and therefore may be considered as having a doubtful claim to the title, "Evidence wholly external."

(4) Some information with respect to dates may be gleaned from the facts that certain companies represented a play, or that it was produced at a certain theatre. Thus the statement on the title-page of the quarto of *Romeo and Juliet*, 1597, that it was acted by "Lord Hunsdon his servants," proves that performances of that play took place between July 22, 1596, and April 1597 (see p. 83). The mention by *Marston* of "*curtain* plaudities" in connection with the same play would have served (had not other positive evidence been forthcoming) to afford a presumption that it was produced at the Curtain Theatre, before 1599, when the Globe was built; for, had the Globe existed when *Romeo and Juliet* first appeared, at the Globe it would probably have been performed.

Such is the evidence for determining the chronology of Shakspere's plays derived from sources lying outside the text of the plays themselves. The evidence in which external and internal elements are united is of two kinds.

27. II. **Evidence partly external partly internal.**—(1) Allusions in the plays to historical events whose date is known.

Thus, in *The Comedy of Errors*, there is a punning allusion (see p. 67) to the civil war in France, which terminated with the submission of Henri IV. to the Catholic Church; the allusion would have had little point if the civil war were not in actual progress. Again, in the chorus prefixed to the last act of *Henry V.*, we read the words:

> Were now the general of our gracious empress,
> (As in good time he may) from Ireland coming,
> Bringing rebellion broached on his sword.

The reference is to the Earl of Essex, who went to Ireland in April, 1599, and returned in the following September. If the choruses were written for the first performance of the play this fixes its date. (See also "the earthquake," *Romeo and Juliet*, p. 83, and the "German Duke," *Merry Wives of Windsor*, p. 104.)

(2) If there be found in a play of Shakspere a quotation from, or allusion to, or matter derived from a book of known date by some other writer, we infer that Shakspere's play was later in date than the book of which use was made by him. In *As You Like It* we have the couplet (Act III. Sc. v. L. 82–83):

> Dead shepherd! now I find thy saw of might—
> "Who ever lov'd that lov'd not at first sight?"

The second line is from Marlowe's *Hero and Leander*, published 1598. Again, in *King Lear* the names of fiends and other portions of the mad speeches put into Edgar's mouth, were derived from Harsnet's *Declaration of egregious Popish Impostures*, 1603. Once more, the description by Gonzalo, in *The Tempest*, of an imaginary commonwealth (Act II. Sc. i. L. 147–156) is taken from Montaigne's *Essays* (Book I. Chap. 30. Of the Caniballes), translated in 1603, by *Florio*; of which translation a copy exists in the British Museum, having the name of Shakspere written in it. The circulation of Elizabethan literature in manuscript should here again be borne in mind as a caution; and it is obvious that while this class of evidence may furnish us with an upward limit, previous to which we cannot place Shakspere's play, it tells us nothing with respect to the downward limit, nor can, by itself, fix the date at which any play was written.

We come now to evidence

28. III. **Wholly Internal.**—And here the great mass of evidence is of a kind which cannot be precisely stated, or definitely weighed and measured; and yet it is not the less real and weighty. As

we do not need a thermometer to inform us of decided changes of temperature in the atmosphere, so we need no scientific test to make us aware that, in passing from *Love's Labour's Lost* to *Hamlet*, and from *Hamlet* to *The Tempest*, we pass from youth to manhood, and again from a manhood of trial and sorrow to the riper manhood of attainment and of calm. Our general impression results from many particulars. We are sensible of a change (*a*) In *the style and diction*. In the earliest plays the language is sometimes as it were a dress put upon the thought —a dress ornamented with superfluous care; the idea is at times hardly sufficient to fill out the language in which it is put; in the middle plays (*Julius Cæsar* serves as an example) there seems a perfect balance and equality between the thought and its expression. In the latest plays this balance is disturbed by the preponderance or excess of the ideas over the means of giving them utterance. The sentences are close-packed; there are "rapid and abrupt turnings of thought, so quick that language can hardly follow fast enough; impatient activity of intellect and fancy, which, having once disclosed an idea, cannot wait to work it orderly out;" "the language is sometimes alive with imagery." (Contrast *Two Gentlemen of Verona*, Act II. Sc. vii. L. 24-38, and its one sweet long-drawn-out image, with such a passage as *Antony and Cleopatra*, Act V. Sc. ii. L. 82-92.) Under this head of style may be noticed Shakspere's early conceits, puns, frequent classical allusions, occasional over-wrought rhetoric (especially in the historical plays), all of which gradually disappear or subside. But these changes really belong to (*b*) The growth of Shakspere's taste and judgment. The Duchess of York, in *Richard II.* (Act V. Sc. iii.), pleads with the king for her son's pardon:

> No word like *pardon* for kings' mouths so meet.

Her husband exclaims:

> Speak it in French, king: say *pardonnez moy*.

This execrable line could not possibly have been written in a play of Shakspere's maturity. (*c*) In the structure of the play and grouping of characters there is, in some of the early plays, a tendency to formal symmetry, an artificial setting of character over against character, and group against group: Antipholus and Dromio against Antipholus and Dromio; Proteus and Launce against Valentine and Speed; the King of Navarre and his three fellow-students against the Princess of France and her three ladies. Afterwards the outline of the play is drawn with a freer because a firmer hand. (*d*) The characterisation changes. At first there are bright and clever sketches of character; sometimes a want of delicacy in the conception of female character; sometimes character is subordinate to incident (as in the *Errors*), or to dialogue (as in *Love's Labour's Lost*). By degrees the characterisation becomes profound and refined. Instead of a Valentine or Demetrius we have a Hamlet or an Othello; instead of a Rosaline, with her bold repartee, we have an Imogen or a Desdemona. (*e*) The entire reflective power deepens; the poet's knowledge of life becomes wider and more varied; his feeling with respect to life, more grave and earnest, for a season, indeed, full of pain and sorrow; at the last, gravely tender, earnest, calm, and harmonious. (*f*) The imagination, which at first worked intermittently, leaving, even in the tragedy of *Romeo and Juliet*, spaces for the fancy to practise its slight devices in, becomes passionately energetic, of daring and all-comprehensive power, as in *King Lear*, or lofty and sustained, with noble ideality, as in *The Tempest*. (*g*) The sympathy with human passion and the power of conceiving and dramatically rendering it in its most massive and most intense forms increases. (*h*) As a result of all this the humour of the dramatist, which was at first comparatively superficial—an enjoyment of amusing absurdity, with pleasure in the keen play of wit—becomes full of grave significance, and works in conjunction with his (*i*) Deepening pathos. It is the transition from Launce and Speed to the sorrowful-eyed Fool of *Lear*. (*j*) Finally, in moral reach, in true justice, in charity, in self-control, in all that indicates fortitude of will, the writings of the mature Shakspere excel, in an extraordinary degree, those of his younger self.

29. **Verse Tests.**—But these are things that cannot be precisely weighed and measured, although they can be clearly felt. There is, however, one kind of internal evidence respecting the chronology of the plays which admits of exact scientific estimation. This evidence is found in the several changes which the verse of Shakspere underwent during his entire dramatic career.

(1) **End-stopt and Run-on Verse.**—Of these changes, that which is most comprehensive and regularly continuous is the transition from unbroken to interrupted verse. At first Shakspere has his breaks and pauses at the end of the line—the verse is "end-stopt;" gradually he more and more found pleasure in carrying on the sense from one line to another without a pause at the end of the line— the verse is "run on," and the breaks and pauses occur with great frequency in some part of the line other than the end. Contrast the following passages, the first from an early play, *The Two Gentlemen of Verona*, the other from a late play, *The Tempest*.

> At Pentecost,
> When all our pageants of delight were play'd,
> Our youth got me to play the woman's part,
> And I was trimmed in Madam Julia's gown,

Which served me as fit, by all men's judgments,
As if the garment had been made for me,
Therefore I know she is about my height.
And at that time I made her weep agood,
For I did play a lamentable part.
(Act IV. Sc. iv. L. 163-171.)

Admired Miranda !
Indeed the top of admiration ! worth
What's dearest to the world ! Full many a lady
I have eyed with best regard, and many a time
The harmony of their tongues hath into bondage
Brought my too diligent ear : for several virtues
Have I liked several women ; never any
With so full soul, but some defect in her
Did quarrel with the noblest grace she owed
And put it to the foil.
(Act III. Sc. i. L. 37-46.)

That these typical passages really illustrate a great general change in the structure of Shakspere's verse appears from the following table, giving "the proportion of run-on lines to end-pause ones in three of the earliest and three of the latest plays of Shakspere."

EARLIEST PLAYS.

	Proportion of unstopt lines to end-stopt ones.
Love's Labour's Lost	1 in 18·14
The Comedy of Errors	1 ,, 10·7
The Two Gentlemen of Verona	1 ,, 10·0

LATEST PLAYS.

	Proportion of unstopt lines to end-stopt ones.
The Tempest	1 in 3·02
Cymbeline	1 ,, 2·52
The Winter's Tale	1 ,, 2·12

(F. J. FURNIVALL.)

"The great superiority of the broken structure is plain, especially for the purposes of dramatic poetry ; it conduces in a marked degree to variety, vivacity, and the natural ease of dialogue;" in the end-stopt style there is, moreover, a frequent temptation to "bumbast out" the blank verse with unnecessary adjectives.

30. (2) **Weak endings.**—Closely related to the change which has now been described, is that which consists in the appearance in Shakspere's verse of weak monosyllabic endings. Two degrees of the weak ending have been distinguished: "On the words which belong to the one of these groups the voice can to a small extent dwell;" the others so precipitate the reader forward that "we are forced to run them, in pronunciation no less than in sense, into the closest connection with the opening words of the succeeding line." The former have been named "light endings," the latter "weak endings." To the former class belong *am, are, be, can, could*; the auxiliaries *do, does, has, had; I, they, thou,* and others: these may be found as terminal words in the blank verse of Milton and of Wordsworth. The latter — the weak endings — are more fugitive and evanescent in character, including such words as *and, for, from, if, in, of, or.* Now weak endings hardly appear in Shakspere's early or middle plays. The *Errors* and *The Two Gentlemen of Verona* do not contain a single light or weak ending; *Midsummer Night's Dream* contains one weak ending; there is one light ending in 2 *Henry IV.*; two light endings in *Henry V.* Nor do they come in by slow degrees at a later period; "the poet seems to have thrown himself at once into this new structure of verse." In *Macbeth* light endings appear for the first time in considerable numbers; weak endings in considerable numbers for the first time in *Antony and Cleopatra.* This test serves perfectly to pick out the plays which form the group belonging to Shakspere's last period of dramatic authorship; and within that period it probably serves to indicate nearly the precise order in which the plays were written. The following table presents the facts with reference to this metrical

peculiarity, from its first appearance in any important degree (in *Macbeth*) until it reaches its maximum in the last plays of Shakspere:

Name of Play.	No. of light endings.	No. of weak endings.	No. of verse lines in play.	Percentage of light endings.	Percentage of weak endings.	Percentage of both together.
Macbeth	21	2	—	—	—	—
Timon	14	?	1112	1·26	?	?
Antony and Cleopatra	71	28	2803	2·53	1·00	3·53
Coriolanus	60	44	2563	2·34	1·71	4·05
Pericles (Sh's. part) .	20	10	719	2·78	1·39	4·17
Tempest	42	25	1460	2·88	1·71	4·59
Cymbeline	78	52	2692	2·90	1·93	4·83
Winter's Tale . . .	57	43	1825	3·12	2·36	5·48
Two Noble Kinsmen (non-Fletcherian part)	50	34	1378	3·63	2·47	6·10
Henry VIII. (Sh's. part)	45	37	1146	3·93	3·23	7·16

(J. K. INGRAM.)

It should be noted that commonly a pause occurs before the weak final monosyllable, after which the verse, as it were, leaps forward. This structure, as has been said, gives to the verse something of the bounding life which Ulysses describes Diomed as showing in the manner of his gait:

> He rises on the toe; that spirit of his
> In aspiration lifts him from the earth.

It conduces to liveliness and variety, and so is hardly appropriate to tragedy of the deeper sort; but it is admirably adapted to the romantic drama of Shakspere's latest stage, and here alone it appears in a conspicuous degree. [See Prof. Ingram's paper on "The Weak endings of Shakspere," *Transactions of New Shak. Soc.* 1874.]

21. (3) **Double (or feminine) endings.**—The next of the indications of date afforded by peculiarities of metre will be found in the rarer or more frequent occurrence of the dissyllabic, or double ending. Stating the fact broadly (for there may be some exceptional plays) if double endings are rare, we may infer that the play is of early date; if they are numerous, that the play is one of Shakspere's middle or later period. Take, again, two typical passages by way of illustration:

> A league from Epidamnum had we sail'd
> Before the always wind-obeying deep
> Gave any tragic instance of our harm:
> But longer did we not retain much hope;
> For what obscured light the heavens did grant
> Did but convey unto our fearful minds
> A doubtful warrant of immediate death.
> (*Comedy of Errors*, Act I. Sc. i. L. 63-69.)

The entire speech of Ægeon, from which this extract is made, consisting of over seventy lines, contains only one certain double ending, line 46. (In lines 52 and 83, "the other" perhaps = th'other.)

> I boarded the king's ship: now on the beak,
> Now in the waist, the deck, in every cab | in
> I flamed amazement: sometimes I'd divide
> And burn in many places; on the top | mast,
> The yards and bowsprit would I flame distinct | ly,
> Then meet and join. Jove's lightnings the precurs | ors
> O' the dreadful thunderclap more momentar | y
> And sight out-running were not; the fire and cracks
> Of sulphurous roaring the most mighty Nep | tune
> Seem to besiege and make his bold waves trem | ble.
> (*The Tempest*, Act I. Sc. ii. L. 196-205.)

Here, again, progress towards dramatic freedom, and a gain of ease and variety, are evident. The slight stress which comes upon the tenth syllable of a blank verse can thus be modified by a kind of gracenote which succeeds it. The following figures give the percentage of double endings in sixteen of Shakspere's plays:

Love's Labour's Lost	4
Titus Andronicus	5
King John	6
Richard II.	11·39
Comedy of Errors	12
Two Gentlemen of Verona	15
Merchant of Venice	15
Taming of the Shrew	16
Richard III.	18
As You Like It	18
Troilus and Cressida	20
All's Well that Ends Well	21
Othello	26
Winter's Tale	31·09
Cymbeline	32
Tempest	33

(HERTZBERG.)

32. (4) **Rhyme.**—Another metrical test of the early or late place of a play is that founded on the frequent or rare occurrence of rhyme. In Shakspere's early comedies there is a very large proportion of rhymed verse. Thus, in *Love's Labour's Lost* there are about two rhymed lines to every one line of blank verse. In *The Comedy of Errors* there are 380 rhymed lines to 1150 unrhymed (*Fleay*). In Shakspere's latest plays there is little or no rhyme. In *The Tempest* two rhymed lines occur; in *The Winter's Tale* not one. These are striking facts, but it must not be hastily inferred that the rhyme test will determine the order of the intermediate plays as well as it serves to indicate the extreme groups. A difference between this metrical characteristic and those previously noticed must be borne in mind, namely, that although a poet may unconsciously set down a double ending or a weak ending, or run on a line into that which follows (this unconscious action serving as an index to the general growth of his artistic powers), he cannot rhyme unconsciously. And we can perceive that Shakspere deliberately employs rhyme for certain definite purposes. It would be an error to conclude that *A Midsummer Night's Dream* preceded *The Comedy of*

Errors because it contains a larger proportion of rhyming lines, until we had first decided whether special incentives to rhyme did not exist in the case of that comedy of Fairyland; and when we meet such a series of ten lines all rhyming together, as that put into Titania's mouth (Act III. Sc. i. L. 168-177), we see that rhyme here is treated with the design of producing special effects. When it is argued that *Richard II.* must be later in date than *Richard III.*, because it contains a far larger proportion of rhymed lines, we should consider whether a special reason for the great predominance of blank verse did not exist in the case of *Richard III.* It was written in continuation of *Henry VI.*, and more than any other play of Shakspere under the influence of the great master of blank verse, Marlowe. In *Richard II.* Shakspere is far more independent of external influence, and he may have been pleased to return to his early manner of rhymed dialogue after a grand experiment in the severer manner of his contemporary. In so late a play as *Othello* we see how Shakspere introduces rhyme to fulfil a special purpose when he sees fit. Thus in Act I. Sc. iii. L. 201-219, to Brabantio, who has lost his daughter, the Duke offers the cold comfort of sententious moralising, comfort wrapped up in little epigrams, each of these epigrams being a rhymed couplet; and Brabantio replies ironically in the same manner. (See also in the same play, Act II. Sc. i. L. 141-169.) Again, in *Troilus and Cressida*, Act IV. Sc. v. L. 28-52, where the Greeks kiss Cressida, there is a flippancy in the speeches which they would lose if turned from rhyme into blank verse. Ulysses' vigorous reprobation of Cressida's conduct, which follows, brings the rhymed passages to a close. Again, the half-play, whole-earnest choosing of a husband by Helena in *All's Well that Ends Well*, Act II. Sc. iii., naturally falls into rhyme. In the same play rhyme is often employed as a vehicle for generalising reflections. We are also bound to consider, in using the rhyme test, not only the numerical proportions of the rhymed and blank verse parts of a play, but the *quality*, the literary merit of the parts. As Shakspere advanced in mastery of blank verse, it would be natural that his greatest scenes should more and more fall into that form. At an earlier time we might expect to find the happiest expression of his genius in the rhymed scenes. Statistics with reference to Shakspere's use of rhyme, and other metrical peculiarities are given in Mr. Fleay's *Shakespearian Manual*, pp. 135, 136. These require verification or correction by a second worker, but are doubtless a valuable approximation to the truth. It must be observed that the ratio of rhyme lines to blank-verse lines fails to indicate the true chronological order of the plays; if, however, those scenes in which no rhyme occurs be set aside, results approaching nearer to what are probably the facts can be obtained; but for this method of using the rhyme test no sufficient reason has been assigned.

33. **Doggerel, &c.**—Doggerel verse, sonnets, and quatrains are not found in plays of late origin.

Two other tests have been suggested and described—the "pause test," by Mr. Spedding (New Shakspere Society's *Transactions*, 1874, p. 26), the "speech-ending test," by Professor Ingram; but they remain to be worked out in detail. The pause test would consist of an analysis of the entire structure of Shakspere's versification at different periods with reference to the distribution of pauses. The speech-ending test would be founded upon an estimate of the proportion of speeches in each play which end with a complete or with a broken line. The broken speech-ending is that preferred in the later plays; the speeches in early plays generally end with a complete line.

CHAPTER V.

PERIODS OF SHAKSPERE'S CAREER. GROUPS AND DATES OF PLAYS.

34. **Four Periods.**—By means of such evidence as has been described in the last chapter we are enabled to determine the precise dates of some of Shakspere's works, in the case of others we can at least approximate to the dates; only in a few cases are we left to conjecture where, within a range of at most some five or seven years, a drama should be placed. Thus, if there is uncertainty here and there in an attempt to assign dates to each particular play, there is little or no uncertainty in naming groups of plays in chronological order, leaving undetermined the order of the plays within those groups.

Shakspere's entire career of authorship extends over twenty years and upwards, beginning about 1588 or 1590, ending about 1612: ten years and upwards lie in the 16th century, ten years and upwards in the 17th. Now the division of the centuries marks roughly a division in the career of Shakspere. About 1601 his genius began to seek new ways; the histories and joyous comedies ceased to be created, and the great series of tragedies was commenced. But each of the decades, which together make up the years of Shakspere's authorship, is itself clearly divisible into two shorter periods: first, from about 1590 to 1595-96, years of dramatic apprenticeship and experiment; secondly, from about 1595-96 to about 1600-1601, the period of the English historical plays and the mirthful and joyous comedies; thirdly, from 1601 to about 1608, the period of grave or bitter comedies and of the great tragedies; last, from about 1608 to 1611 or

1613, the period of the romantic plays, which are at once grave and glad, serene and beautiful poems, like *The Tempest* and *The Winter's Tale.* These four periods may be designated with reference to the class of works written in each, or with reference to the subjects of those works, or with reference to the kind of versification which was characteristic of each period, or with reference to Shakspere's supposed condition and state of mind in each. I think the reader will remember the following names of the four periods, which may seem fanciful, yet which perhaps convey as much true information as any others: I will call the first period, "In the workshop;" the second, "In the world;" the third, "Out of the depths;" the fourth, "On the heights." The significance of these names will appear as we proceed.

35. **Groups of Plays. Pre-Shaksperian Group.**—Now let us go farther, and try to make out groups of Shakspere's plays in chronological order. Shakspere began his apprenticeship by re-handling plays which were not his. Of such work we have examples in *Titus Andronicus* and the *First Part of Henry VI.*, plays of blood, bombast, and fire, pre-Shaksperian in spirit, but showing touches of that hand which even in its apprentice years was capable of master touches. These two plays we name (i.) the "pre-Shaksperian group."

36. **Early Comedy.**—Next, the young dramatist went to work on his own account, and began to experiment in different kinds of comedy. *Love's Labour's Lost* is full of a young man's thought, wit, and satire, a comedy of oddities, of dialogue carefully elaborated and pointed (as dialogue in a first original work would be), and underlying this a young man's theory with reference to culture and education; *The Comedy of Errors* is a comedy of incident, almost a farce; *The Two Gentlemen of Verona* is a first and somewhat slight experiment in the same kind of love-comedy of which Shakspere afterwards created so many delightful

examples; *A Midsummer Night's Dream* is bright with the poetry of a young man's fancy: in Theseus there is a fine sketch of heroic character, and in Bottom and his companions we find Shakspere's richest humorous work of this period. Whether *The Two Gentlemen of Verona* or *A Midsummer Night's Dream* was written first cannot be decided. This group of four plays we name (ii.) "Early Comedy."

37. **Early History. Poems.**—While engaged upon this group Shakspere's powers as a rising playwright must have been recognised; before he had completed it *Venus and Adonis* was published. When *Chettle* wrote in 1592, Shakspere had already gained the patronage of powerful friends. It is probable that while engaged on his early comedies, Shakspere (continuing to re-handle dramas for the stage) set about the revision of the old historical plays, *The Contention* and *The True Tragedy*, and was assisted by *Marlowe*, one of the original authors of the old plays. Thus came the *Second* and *Third Parts of Henry VI.* to be written, and the character of Richard in those plays was recognised by Shakspere as so admirable a creation for dramatic purposes, that he proceeded to a new play, of which he was sole author, in which Richard should be the principal, one might almost say the only actor. *Richard III.* was a character so essentially Marlowesque, and Shakspere had been so lately working in conjunction with that great poet, that he carried on the Marlowesque spirit from *Henry VI.* into his own play. This group of three plays we name (iii.) "Early History," and must add a second title, "the Marlowe-Shakspere group," finding in the *Second* and *Third Parts of Henry VI.* Marlowe's presence, and in *Richard III.* (almost more dominant than his presence) Marlowe's influence. To this period belongs the *Lucrece*.

38. **Early Tragedy.**—From an early date Shakspere seems to have designed a tragedy; not one of the bloody school of the pre-Shaksperians,

not one like *The Jew of Malta* or *The Spanish Tragedy*, but in which sorrow and beauty should blend and become one. *Romeo and Juliet* may have been begun or written in a first form at the same time as some of the early comedies. I do not think it received its final form until about 1596, but fragments of an earlier date remain in the play. This, if we set aside *Titus Andronicus*, was Shakspere's first tragedy. It is, in its beauty, its passion, and its defects, characteristically a young man's achievement, the lyrical tragedy of youth, of love, and of death: it stands by itself, and we name it (iv.) "Early Tragedy."

39. **Middle History.**—After the Marlowesque *Richard III.*, which completes the series of four historical plays concerned with the fortunes of the house of York, Shakspere turned to the closely-connected subject of the fortunes of the house of Lancaster, and began a new series of historical plays with *Richard II.* He was determined now to try his own dramatic methods and manner in history, and so there is much rhyme in *Richard II.* But the play is of a more complex structure than *Richard III.*, and the characterisation is more subtle and more varied. To the same period belongs *King John*. The advantage taken of a humorous element, appearing here in the person of Faulconbridge, gives us a foretaste of the blending of comedy with history, which was afterwards brought to perfection in *Henry IV.* We name this group of two plays (v.) "Middle History."

40. **Middle Comedy.**—To about the same date as *King John* belongs *The Merchant of Venice*. It stands midway between the early and the later comedies, and partakes of the characteristics of both groups. (See p. 91.) We name it (vi.) "Middle Comedy."

41. **Later History.**—Having treated history and comedy separately, the next step was to unite them.

Henry IV., Parts I. and *II.*, are the comedy of Falstaff as much as they are the history of the troublesome times of the king. *The Merry Wives of Windsor* may have been sketched at an earlier date; it is not impossible that it assumed its present form at a later date; but upon the whole the evidence inclines us to place it here, Shakspere hastily dashing off the prose play to comply with a command of the Queen, who desired to see Falstaff in love. (See p. 103.) The date of *The Taming of the Shrew* is also uncertain, some critics placing it as late as 1602–1603 or later (which seems incredible), some as early as 1594. In its rough and boisterous mirth it has affinities with *The Merry Wives*, and perhaps lies close to it in the chronological order. Certainty upon this point is fortunately not of great importance, for only a portion of *The Taming of the Shrew* is by Shakspere, and that portion, though full of vigour and high spirits, is as much a farce as a comedy. In the series of histories *Henry V.* follows close upon *Henry IV., Part II.* In it Shakspere pictured his ideal king, and bade farewell, in trumpet notes, to English history. For convenience here, where so little disturbance of the chronological order is caused, it is well to connect *The Merry Wives* and *The Shrew* with the comedies which follow, and to bring together the *Second* and *Third Parts Henry IV.* and *Henry V.*, which group we name (vii.) "Later History."

42. **Later Comedy.**—A series of comedies follows, and as the series was started before the histories had come to an end, so its later plays overlap the subsequent tragedies. It might indeed be desirable to make the fact prominent, by placing the last three comedies in a group by themselves, later than *Julius Cæsar* and *Hamlet*. If, however, the student will bear in mind that this group runs on and overlaps the tragedies, something will be gained, from a logical point of view, by keeping the comedies together, and

allowing *Julius Cæsar* and *Hamlet* to stand near the great tragedies of later date, with which they may be compared and contrasted.

(*a*) The earliest of these comedies are, then, *The Shrew* and *The Merry Wives*, somewhat rough and boisterous plays, written with high spirit, entirely free from the presence of pain or sorrow. But such rough humour was not after Shakspere's own heart at this time. *The Merry Wives* was a task imposed upon him, which he executed with a hearty energy; but still it was not a work of his own choice. *The Shrew* also was but half his own, for he was forced to preserve the tone of the farce-like piece upon which he worked. But in the plays which immediately follow, the true Shaksperian comedy reaches its utmost beauty and perfection. (*b*) In *Much Ado about Nothing*, the high spirits which had given life to *The Shrew* and *The Merry Wives* still play their part, in a more excellent way, in the creation of the brilliant pair, Beatrice and Benedick. Everything grows finer, more harmonious, more sweetly tempered in the pastoral comedy, *As You Like It*. But the discontent of a superficial critic of life, breathing through the glades of Arden, the melancholy of Jaques, is like the first touch of autumn wind upon the leaves, which to our sense may have a pleasant poignancy, yet which foretells the approach of the sad and barren days. In *Twelfth Night* this passes away; and, upon the whole, if there be any presence of sadness in these beautiful and happy plays, it is a musical sadness which is resolved into a fuller harmony of joy. *Twelfth Night* brings us to the opening of the 17th century, and now Shakspere began his great series of tragedies with *Julius Cæsar*. Continuing, however, to trace the comedies, we next come to three which present a striking contrast to those which have just been named. (*c*) *All's Well that Ends Well* closes happily, as the title implies, but it is not a bright and sunny play; it is earnest, and serious in parts, and the strong-willed heroine, who feels the earnestness of life and love, though she is noble, has not the romantic charm of a Viola or a Rosalind. In *Measure for Measure* a dark and evil world is pictured, and out of this emerge the strength and purity of Isabella, one of Shakspere's highest conceptions of female character, but, like Helena, deficient in charm. It is as if Shakspere at this time were writing comedy when he ought to have been engaged on tragedy, and creating characters in heroic mould which in comedy hardly find their fitting places. Deep thoughts on life and death in *Measure for Measure* remind us of *Hamlet*, and the sin, the soul-searching of Angelo, his abasement and discovery of guilt we scrutinise with a painful interest. I would place *Troilus and Cressida* here, and in it we reach a still greater distance from the spirit of true comedy. It is the comedy of disillusion. The young enthusiasm of Troilus is miserably disenchanted. Ulysses has come to accept all the baseness of life as part of the nature of things, and as material to be turned to account by worldly wisdom. Thersites spews over everything that we had deemed high and sacred, his foul, yet not all unwarrantable insults. Cressida is a shallow-hearted wanton. Having reached this point, Shakspere could not but cease for a time to write comedy.

This series of eight plays we group together, and name them (viii.) "Later Comedy." But the entire series of eight divides itself into three smaller groups: the first—two plays of rough and boisterous mirth; the second—three comedies almost purely joyous, romantic and refined; the third—three comedies, one earnest, another dark and severe, the last, bitter and ironical.

43. **Middle Tragedy.**—Shakspere's first tragedy was a lyrical tragedy of youth, of love, and of death. When, after completing his series of historical plays and his joyous comedies, Shakspere again turned to tragic themes, he wrote as a man of mature powers, and as a thinker. In his histories he had been dealing with the real world, the world of action. In

his two tragedies, *Julius Cæsar* and *Hamlet*, he studies the failure in practical affairs of two men, Brutus and Hamlet, who are called to the performance of great actions, but who are disqualified, the one for acting wisely, the other for acting energetically. Hamlet and Brutus fail, yet we honour them; they fall as martyrs or victims to duties imposed upon them as it were by fate, and which become burdens too heavy for them to bear. These two tragedies are tragedies of reflection; Shakspere is not yet caught up in the passionate wind of his own imagination. Everything is thought out and wrought out deliberately in these two plays. We name this group (ix.) "Middle Tragedy."

44. **Later Tragedy.**—The tragedies of passion follow. Error and misfortune, or, at worst, weakness or indiscretion, had ruined the lives of Brutus and Hamlet. They had not wronged their own souls by crime. But now passion and crime form the subjects of tragedy, instead of error or the cruelty of fate. The bonds of life are broken: in *Othello*, the bonds which unite husband and wife; in *Lear*, the bonds which unite parent and child; in *Macbeth*, the bonds of kinship and of the loyalty of the subject; Antony, through voluptuous self-indulgence, dissolves the bonds which bind him to his country, and ceases to be a Roman; Coriolanus, through passionate haughtiness, also turns away from Rome, and even tries to crush the loyalties and affections which make him man—tries to lift himself into a proud isolation; lastly, Timon actually severs himself, not from his country merely, but from humanity itself. He is "misanthropos, and hates mankind." But he is not formed for misanthropy, and is slain by his unnatural hatred. This group of plays we name (x.) "Later Tragedy."

45. **Romances.**—The transition from these to Shakspere's last plays is most remarkable. From the tragic passion which reached its climax in *Timon of*

Athens, we suddenly pass to beauty and serenity; from the plays concerned with the violent breaking of human bonds, to a group of plays which are all concerned with the knitting together of human bonds, the reunion of parted kindred, the forgiveness of enemies, the atonement for wrong—not by death but by repentance—the reconciliation of husband with wife, of child with father, of friend with friend. *Pericles* is a sketch in which only a part of the subject of these last plays is clearly conceived; it is in some respects like a slighter and earlier *Tempest*, in which Lord Cerimon is the Prospero. It also contains hints afterwards worked out in *The Winter's Tale*; the reunion of the Prince of Tyre and his lost Thaisa is a kind of anticipation of the re-discovery by Leontes of his wife whom he had so long believed to be dead. Posthumus's jealousy, his perception of his error, his sorrow, and his pardon, may be contrasted with the similar series of incidents in *The Winter's Tale*, and the exquisitely impulsive and generous Imogen may be set over against the grave, statue-like Hermione, whose forgiveness follows the long years of suffering, endured with noble fortitude. Prospero is also wronged; his enemies are in his power; but he has employed his supernatural ministers to lead them to penitence rather than to bring them to punishment. He has learned that "the rarer action is in virtue than in vengeance." In these plays there are two sets of *dramatis personæ*: the great sufferers, aged and experienced—Pericles, Prospero, Hermione, afterwards Queen Katherine; and the young and beautiful children in the brightness of the morning of life—Miranda, Perdita, Arviragus, and Guiderius; and Shakspere seems to render homage to both: to the great sufferers for their virtue, and patience, and sorrow; to the young men and maidens for their beauty and their joy. There is a romantic element about these plays. In all there is the same romantic incident of lost children recovered by those to whom they are dear—the daughters of Pericles and Leontes, the sons of Cymbeline and Alonso. In all there is a beautiful romantic background of sea or mountain. The dramas have a grave beauty, a sweet serenity, which seem to render the name "comedies" inappropriate; we may smile tenderly, but we never laugh loudly, as we read them. Let us, then, name this group, consisting of four plays, (xi.) Romances.

46. **Fragments.**—There only remain the two (xii.) fragments of *Henry VIII.* and *The Two Noble Kinsmen.* The same spirit appears in these as in the Romances. In each of these plays the work of Shakspere is united with that of Fletcher.

47. **Summary.**—The following table presents the series of groups in chronological order, as they have been here made out; the plays in each group are arranged in what is supposed to be the true order of succession; and the date of each play (ascertained or conjectured) is affixed.

1. PRE-SHAKSPERIAN GROUP.

(*Touched by Shakspere.*)

Titus Andronicus (1588-90).
1 Henry VI. (1590-91).

2. EARLY COMEDIES.

Love's Labour's Lost (1590).
Comedy of Errors (1591).
Two Gentlemen of Verona (1592-93).
Midsummer Night's Dream (1593-94).

3. MARLOWE-SHAKSPERE GROUP.

EARLY HISTORY.

2 & 3 Henry VI. (1591-92).
Richard III. (1593).

4. EARLY TRAGEDY.

Romeo and Juliet (? two dates, 1591, 1596-97).

5. MIDDLE HISTORY.

Richard II. (1594).
King John (1595).

6. MIDDLE COMEDY.

Merchant of Venice (1596).

7. LATER HISTORY.

History and Comedy united.

1 & 2 Henry IV. (1597-98).
Henry V. (1599).

8. LATER COMEDY.

(*a*) *Rough and boisterous Comedy.*

Taming of the Shrew (? 1597).
Merry Wives (? 1598).

(*b*) *Joyous, refined, romantic.*
Much Ado about Nothing (1598).
As You Like It (1599).
Twelfth Night (1600-1601).

(*c*) *Serious, dark, ironical.*
All's Well (? 1601-1602).
Measure for Measure (1603).
Troilus and Cressida (? 1603; revised 1607?).

9. MIDDLE TRAGEDY.
Julius Cæsar (1601).
Hamlet (1602).

10. LATER TRAGEDY.
Othello (1604).
Lear (1605).
Macbeth (1606).

Antony and Cleopatra (1607).
Coriolanus (1608).
Timon (1607-1608).

11. ROMANCES.
Pericles (1608).
Cymbeline (1609).
Tempest (1610).
Winter's Tale (1610-11).

12. FRAGMENTS.
Two Noble Kinsmen (1612).
Henry VIII. (1612-13).

POEMS.
Venus and Adonis (? 1592).
Lucrece (1593-94.)
Sonnets (? 1595-1605).

48. **Plots of Comedies.**—The student will observe in this arrangement, early, middle, and later Comedy; early, middle, and later History; and early, middle, and later Tragedy. Not only is it well to view the entire body of Shakspere's plays in the order of their chronological succession, but also to trace in chronological order the three separate lines of Comedy, History, and Tragedy. The group named Romances connect themselves, of course, with the Comedies; but there is a grave element in them which is connected with the Tragedies which preceded them. It has been noticed that the Romances have in common the incidents of reunions, reconciliations, and the recovery of lost children. Shakspere, though so remarkable for his power of creating character, is not distinguished among dramatists by his power of inventing incident. Having found a situation which interested his imagination, or was successful on the stage, he introduced it again and

again, with variations. Thus, in the Early Comedies, mistakes of identity, disguises, errors, and bewilderments, in various forms, recur as a source of merriment and material for adventure. In the Later Comedies, again, it is quite remarkable how Shakspere (generally in the portions of these plays which are due to his own invention) repeats, with variations, the incident of a trick or fraud practised upon one who is a self-lover, and its consequences, grave or gay. Thus Falstaff is fatuous enough to believe that two English matrons are dying of love for him, and is made the victim of their merry tricks. Malvolio is made an ass of by the mischievous Maria taking advantage of his solemn self-esteem; Beatrice and Benedick are cunningly entrapped, through their good-natured vanity, into love for which they had been already predisposed; the boastful Parolles is deceived, flouted, and disgraced by his fellow-soldiers; and (Shakspere's mood growing earnest, and his thoughts being set upon deep questions of character) Angelo, the self-deceiver, by the craft of the Duke, is discovered painfully to the eyes of others and to his own heart.

49. **First Period.**—Returning now from our more detailed classification, let us glance once again at the four periods into which we divided Shakspere's career of authorship. The first, which I named *In the workshop*, was the period during which Shakspere was learning his trade as a dramatic craftsman. Starting at the age of twenty-four or twenty-six, he made rapid progress, and cannot but have been aware of this. The works of Shakspere's youth—experiments in various directions—are all marked by the presence of vivacity, cleverness, delight in beauty, and a quick enjoyment of existence. If an industrious apprentice, he was also a gay and courageous one.

50. **Second Period.**—As yet, however, he wrote with small experience of human life; the early plays are slight or fanciful, rather than real and massive. But now

Shakspere's imagination began to lay hold of real life; he came to understand the world and the men in it; his plays begin to deal in an original and powerful way with the matter of history. "The compression of the large and rough matter of history into dramatic form demanded vigorous exercise of the plastic energy of the imagination; and the circumstance that he was dealing with reality and positive facts of the world, must have served to make clear to Shakspere that there was sterner stuff of poetry, material more precious —even for purposes of art—in actual life, than could be found in the conceits, and prettinesses, and affectations which at times led him astray in his earlier writings." During this period Shakspere's work grows strong and robust. It was the time when he was making rapid advance in worldly prosperity, and accumulating the fortune on which he meant to retire as a country gentleman. I name the second period therefore *In the world*.

51. **Third Period**.—Before it closed Shakspere had known sorrow: his son was dead; his father died probably soon after Shakspere had written his *Twelfth Night*; his friend of the *Sonnets* had done him wrong. Whatever the cause may have been, the fact seems certain that the poet now ceased to care for tales of mirth and love, for the stir and movement of history, for the pomp of war; he needed to sound, with his imagination, the depths of the human heart; to inquire into the darkest and saddest parts of human life; to study the great mystery of evil. The belief in human virtue, indeed, never deserts him: in *Lear* there is a Cordelia; in *Macbeth* a Banquo; even Troilus will be the better, not the worse, for his disenchantment with Cressida; and it is because Timon would fain love that he is driven to hate. Still, during this period, Shakspere's genius left the bright surface of the world, and was at work in the very heart and centre of things. I have named it *Out of the depths*.

52. Fourth Period.—The tragic gloom and suffering were not, however, to last for ever. The dark cloud lightens and rolls away, and the sky appears purer and tenderer than ever. The impression left upon the reader by Shakspere's last plays is that, whatever his trials and sorrows and errors may have been, he had come forth from them wise, large-hearted, calm-souled. He seems to have learned the secret of life, and while taking his share in it, to be yet disengaged from it; he looks down upon life, its joys, its griefs, its errors, with a grave tenderness, which is almost pity. The spirit of these last plays is that of serenity which results from fortitude, and the recognition of human frailty; all of them express a deep sense of the need of repentance and the duty of forgiveness. And they all show a delight in youth and the loveliness of youthful joy, such as one feels who looks on these things without possessing or any longer desiring to possess them. Shakspere in this period is most like his own Prospero. In these "Romances," and in the "Fragments," a supernatural element is present; man does not strive with circumstance and with his own passions in darkness; the gods preside over our human lives and fortunes, they communicate with us by vision, by oracles, through the elemental powers of nature. Shakspere's faith seems to have been that there is something without and around our human lives, of which we know little, yet which we know to be beneficent and divine. And it will be felt that the name which I have given to this last period—Shakspere having ascended out of the turmoil and trouble of action, out of the darkness and tragic mystery, the places haunted by terror and crime, and by love contending with these, to a pure and serene elevation —it will be felt that the name, *On the heights*, is neither inappropriate nor fanciful.

CHAPTER VI.

INTRODUCTIONS TO THE PLAYS AND POEMS.

1. **Titus Andronicus** (pronounced by the writer of the play Andrŏn'-ĭ-cus).—The importance of this tragedy lies in the fact that, if Shakspere wrote it, we find him as a young man carried away by the influence of a *Sturm und Drang* (storm and stress) movement similar to that which urged Schiller to write his *Robbers*. *Titus Andronicus* belongs essentially to the pre-Shaksperian group of bloody tragedies, of which Kyd's *Spanish Tragedy* is the most conspicuous example. If it is of Shaksperian authorship it may be viewed as representing the years of crude and violent youth before he had found his true self; his second tragedy, *Romeo and Juliet*, as representing the years of transition; and *Hamlet*, the period of maturity and adult power.

The external evidence with reference to the authorship of *Titus* is the following: (1) It is mentioned by Meres (1598) among other undoubted plays of Shakspere. (2) It is printed in the First Folio. (3) *Ravenscroft*, who altered the play in 1687, declares that he had been told "by some anciently conversant with the stage that it was not his [Shakspere's]," but that he only gave "some master-touches to one or two of the principal parts or characters." The great majority of English critics either altogether reject the play, upon the ground that in style and subject it is unlike any other work of our dramatist, or accept as true the tradition of *Ravenscroft*, that it was touched by Shakspere, and no more. "Shakspere's tragedy is never bloodily sensual; . . . this play is a perfect slaughterhouse, and the blood makes appeal to all the senses. . . . It reeks blood, it smells of blood, we almost feel that we have handled blood—it is so gross." To attempt to point out certain passages as written by Shakspere would be unsafe, for we know little of what the distinguishing features of Shakspere's style were when he began to write for the stage; but no lines in the play have more of a Shaksperian ring than the following (Act IV. Sc. iv. L. 81–86):

> King, be thy thoughts imperious, like thy name.
> Is the sun dimm'd that gnats do fly in it?
> The eagle suffers little birds to sing,
> And is not careful what they mean thereby,
> Knowing that with the shadow of his wings
> He can at pleasure stint their melody.

A play, *Titus and Vespasian* (mentioned by Henslowe as "tittus and vespacia"), was acted in 1592, and though itself lost, a translation into German, acted early in the 17th century by English comedians in Germany, remains in existence. It is not the play attributed to Shakspere. Henslowe also mentions a *Titus and Andronicus* as a new play, acted January 23, 1594: it is doubtful whether this was the Shaksperian play. If it be, and it was then written, the tragedy is certainly not by Shakspere. It is impossible to believe that in 1594, when Shakspere had written his *Venus and Adonis* and his *Lucrece*, he could have dealt so coarsely with details of outrage and unnatural cruelty as does the author of this tragedy. Ben Jonson, in the introduction to *Bartholomew Fair* (1614), speaks of *Titus Andronicus*, with *Jeronimo*, as belonging to "twenty-five or thirty years" previously: this would carry back the date of the play (if it be of this *Titus Andronicus* that Jonson speaks) to 1589, or earlier. That it was a play of that period, and was touched by Shakspere, we may accept as the opinion best supported by internal evidence and by the weight of critical authority.

2. **King Henry VI., Part I.,** is almost certainly an old play, by one or more authors, which, as we find

it in the First Folio, had received touches from the hand of Shakspere. In Henslowe's diary a *Henry VI.* is said to have been acted March 3, 1591-92. It was extremely popular. Nash in his *Pierce Pennilesse* (1592) alludes to the triumph on the stage of "brave Talbot" over the French. But we have no reason for believing that the play which we possess was that mentioned by Henslowe or that alluded to by Nash. Greene had, perhaps, a chief hand in this play, and he may have been assisted by Peele and Marlowe. There is a general agreement among critics in attributing to Shakspere the scene (Act II. Sc. iv.) in which the white and red roses are plucked as emblems of the rival parties in the state; perhaps the scene of the wooing of Margaret by Suffolk (Act V. Sc. iii. L. 45 and onwards) if not written by Shakspere was touched by him. The general spirit of the drama belongs to an older school than the Shaksperian, and it is a happiness not to have to ascribe to our greatest poet the crude and hateful handling of the character of Joan of Arc, excused though to some extent it may be by the concurrence of view in our old English chronicles.

3. **Love's Labour's Lost**, as far as we know, is wholly of Shakspere's own invention; no source of the plot has been discovered. The play is precisely such an one as a clever young man might imagine, who had come lately from the country—with its "daisies pied and violets blue," its "merry larks," its maidens who "bleach their summer smocks," its pompous parish schoolmaster, and its dull constable (a great public official in his own eyes)—to the town, where he was surrounded by more brilliant unrealities, and affectations of dress, of manner, of language, and of ideas. *Love's Labour's Lost* is a dramatic plea on behalf of nature and of common sense against all that is unreal and affected. It maintains, in a gay and witty fashion, the superiority of life, as a means of education, over books; the superiority of the large world into which

we are born over any little world we can construct for ourselves, and into which we may hedge ourselves by rule ; and, while maintaining this, it also asserts that we must not educate ourselves only by what is mirthful and pleasant in the world, but must recognise its sorrow, and that we cannot be rightly glad without being grave and earnest. The King of Navarre, and three of his lords—one of whom, Berowne, sees through the seeming splendour of the king's design to its real folly—resolve to turn their court into a "little Academe," to seclude themselves from all that is common and unideal, to devote themselves for three years to study, fasting much, sleeping little, and forswearing the company of ladies : in a word, they aspire to establish a little monastery of culture. The scheme, which looked so graceful while it went no farther than words, breaks down lamentably when they would make it real. The king is obliged, by reasons of state, to receive the Princess of France and her three ladies ; the vowed scholars—all four of them—fall over head and ears in love, and an amusing scene of discovery and confession takes place, in which each in turn betrays his secret, and is convicted before his equally guilty fellows, until at last Berowne—who unites good sense with genius—comes forward to charge with error their original vows of seclusion, and to justify their present apostasy. There is much merry mocking of the lovers by the French girls, and in bright play with the weapons of words Rosaline is a match for Berowne. When the mirth is at its highest come tidings that the father of the princess is dead. The comedy will not end with weddings ; love's labour is lost ; the king is dismissed to a twelvemonth's absence and testing of his love ; and Berowne, the mocker, in the same interval before marriage, must make his jests, if he can, for sick folk in an hospital, and so learn the graver side of life. Thus, with its apparent lightness, there is a serious spirit underlying the play, but the surface is all jest, and stir, and sparkle. It is a comedy of dialogue rather than of incident, and in the persons of Don Adriano de Armado, a fantastical Spaniard, of Sir Nathaniel the curate, and of Holofernes the schoolmaster, are caricatured various Elizabethan absurdities of speech, pseudo-refinement, and pseudo-learning. The braggart soldier and the pedant are characters well known in Italian comedy, and perhaps it was from that quarter that the hint came to Shakspere, which stirred his imagination to create these ridiculous figures. Holofernes, some persons have supposed to be a satirical sketch of an individual—John Florio, author of an Italian dictionary; but Shakspere did not in any ascertained instances satirise individual persons, and there is little evidence in this case to warrant the supposition. The fifth act winds up with a pair of songs in the most genuine country style, rustic yet graceful, such songs as the milkmaids of Isaac Walton might sing. After the daintinesses, and pomposities, and affectations, come these fresh rural ditties. The play contains nothing which serves to ascertain its precise date, but it certainly belongs to Shakspere's earliest dramatic period. The first quarto was printed in 1598 (probably in the spring of the year 1598-99) " as it was presented before her Highness [Queen Elizabeth] this last Christmas [probably the Christmas of 1598], Newly corrected and augmented." Two traces of the alterations from the original play may still be observed. In Act V. Sc. ii., the lines 827–832 ought not to appear, being almost certainly the fragment of the play in its first form, which was afterwards worked out in the lines 833–879. Similarly in Berowne's great speech, Act IV. Sc. iii., the lines 296–317 contain passages which are repeated or altered in the lines which follow, 318–354, and obviously some of the lines of the original version have here been retained through a mistake.

4. **The Comedy of Errors** is Shakspere's one farcical play. Its sources of laughter lie almost wholly in the situations and incidents, hardly at all in the charac-

ters. The spectator of the play is called on to accept much that is improbable and all but impossible, not as in *A Midsummer Night's Dream*, for the sake of freer play of imagination, and because the world pictured by the poet is a fairy-world of romantic beauty and grotesqueness, but for the sake of mere fun and laughter-stirring surprises. So cleverly, however, are the incidents and persons entangled and disentangled, so rapidly does surprise follow surprise, that we are given no time to raise difficulties and offer objections. The subject of the comedy is the same as that of the *Menæchmi* of Plautus—mistakes of identity arising from the likeness of twin-born children. How Shakspere made acquaintance with Plautus we are not certain; possibly through William Warner's translation of the *Menæchmi*, seen in manuscript before its publication in 1595; more probably through an earlier play, not now extant, perhaps that one which was acted in 1576 at Hampton Court, under the name of *The Historie of Error*. The hint for Act III. Sc. i., where Antipholus of Ephesus is shut out from his own house while his brother and wife are at dinner within, seems to have been taken from the *Amphitruo* of Plautus, where Jupiter, the supposed Amphitruo, takes possession of the house of the real Amphitruo, and beguiles its mistress. To the twins of the *Menæchmi* are added, by Shakspere, their servants, a second pair of brothers, the twins Dromio. This does not make the improbability of the whole seem greater, but rather the reverse; for the fun is doubled, and where so much is incredible we are carried away and have no wish but to yield ourselves up to belief in the incredible for the time being, so as to enter thoroughly into the jest. Shakspere added other characters—the Duke Solinus (when he can he always introduces a duke), Ægeon, Balthazar, Angelo, the Abbess, and Luciana, and he alters the character of the married brother, Antipholus, from the repulsive Menæchmus of Plautus, with whom we can have little sympathy, into a person who at least is not base and vicious. The scene he transfers from Epidamnum to Ephesus, that city which had an evil repute for its roguery, licentiousness, and magical practices, a city in which such *errors* might be supposed to be the result of sorcery and witchcraft. (See Act I. Sc. ii. L. 97-102.) To Shakspere belongs wholly the serious background, from which the farcical incidents stand out in relief—the story of the Syracusan merchant who almost forfeits his life in the search for his lost children, and finally recovers both the lost ones and his own liberty. There is a fine passage, full of pathos, and almost in Shakspere's later dramatic manner, where the old man, a prisoner before the duke, finds that his son does not recognise his face, nor remember his voice (Act V. Sc. i. L. 295-322); but such passages, in which character or human passion rather than incident chiefly interests us, are rare. As the twins Antipholus are indistinguishable in person and costume, so there is little or no attempt made to discriminate their characters; the Dromios are only a pair of jesters, alike and equally serviceable for receiving hard knocks and returning witty answers. But Adriana, the jealous wife, has some individuality; she is more than an excuse for ridiculous accidents; Shakspere takes some interest in doing her dramatic justice; her shrewish temper is that of a woman who loves her husband, and who would persecute him into loving only her. The date of the play cannot be exactly determined, but it is certainly one of the very earliest plays. "In what part of her body stands.... France?" asks Antipholus of Syracuse, questioning Dromio about the kitchen-wench, who is so large and round that she has been compared to a globe: and Dromio answers: "In her forehead, armed and reverted, making war against her *heir*." (Act III. Sc. ii. L. 125-27.) France was in a state of civil war, fighting for and against her heir, Henri IV., from August, 1589, until shortly before his coronation, in February, 1594. In 1591 Henri received the assistance of troops from England, commanded by the Earl of Essex.

5. **The Two Gentlemen of Verona**, though in parts slightly worked out, exhibits an advance on the preceding comedies. The *Errors* was a clever tangle of diverting incidents, with a few passages of lyric beauty, and one of almost tragic pathos; *Love's Labour's Lost* was a play of glittering and elaborate dialogue. In *The Two Gentlemen of Verona* Shakspere struck into a new path, which he was to pursue with admirable results; it is his earliest comedy in which a romantic love-story is told in dramatic form. Here first Shakspere records the tender and passionate history of a woman's heart, and the adventures to which love may prompt her. Julia (who is like a crayon sketch of Juliet, conceived in a way suitable to comedy instead of tragedy) is the first of that charming group of children of Shakspere's imagination which includes Viola, Portia, Rosalind, and Imogen—women who assume, under some constraint of fortune, the disguise of male attire, and who, while submitting to their transformation, forfeit none of the grace, the modesty, the sensitive delicacy, or the pretty wilfulness of their sex. Launce, accompanied by his immortal dog, leads the train of Shakspere's humorous clowns: his rich, grotesque humanity is "worth all the bright, fantastic interludes of Boyet and Adriano, Costard and Holofernes," worth all the "dancing doggerel or broad-witted prose of either Dromio." The play contains a number of sketches, from which Shakspere afterwards worked out finished pictures. (See p. 91, *Merchant of Venice*.) The characters are clearly conceived, and contrasted with almost too obvious a design: the faithful Valentine is set over against the faithless Proteus; the bright and clever Silvia is set over against the tender and ardent Julia; the clown Speed, notable as a verbal wit and quibbler, is set over against the humorous Launce.

The general theme of the play we may define as love and friendship, with their mutual relations. The *dénouement* in Act V., if written by Shakspere in the form we now have it, is a very crude piece of work. Proteus' sudden repentance, Valentine's sudden abandonment to him of Silvia, under an impulse of extravagant friendship ("all that was mine in Silvia I give thee;" Act V. Sc. iv. L. 83), and Silvia's silence and passiveness whilst disposed of from lover to lover, are, even for the fifth act of a comedy, strangely unreal and ill-contrived. Can it be that this fifth act has reached us in an imperfect form, and that some speeches between Silvia and Valentine have dropped out? The date of the play cannot be definitely fixed; but its place among the comedies is probably after *Love's Labour's Lost*, and before *A Midsummer Night's Dream*. The language and verse are characterised by an even sweetness; rhymed lines and doggerel verses are lessening in number; the blank verse is written with careful regularity. It is as if Shakspere were giving up his early licences of versification, were aiming at a more refined style (which occasionally became a little tame), but being still a novice in the art of writing blank verse, were timid, and failed to write it with the freedom and "happy valiancy" which distinguish his later manner. The story of *The Two Gentlemen of Verona* is identical in many particulars with *The Story of the Shepherdess Felismena*, in the Spanish pastoral romance, *Diana*, by George of Montemayor; but though manuscript translations of the *Diana* existed at an earlier date, no translation was published before that of Yonge, in 1598. The story had probably been dramatised before Shakspere's play, for we read in the accounts of the revels of *The History of Felix and Philomena*, acted before her Highness in 1584. Valentine's consenting to become captain of the robbers has been compared with a somewhat similar incident in Sidney's

Arcadia, but the coincidences are slight, and it may be doubted that Shakspere had here any thought of the *Arcadia*.

6. **A Midsummer Night's Dream** is a strange and beautiful web, woven delicately by a youthful poet's fancy. What is perhaps most remarkable about the play is the harmonious blending in it of widely different elements. It is as if threads of silken splendour were run together in its texture with a yarn of hempen homespun, and both these with lines of dewy gossamer and filaments drawn from the moonbeams. In North's *Plutarch*, or in Chaucer's *Knight's Tale*, Shakspere may have found the figures of Theseus and his Amazonian bride; from Chaucer also (*Wife of Bath's Tale*), may have come the figure of the elf-queen (though not her name, Titania), and the story of Pyramus and Thisbe (see Chaucer's *Legend of Good Women*); this last, however, was perhaps taken from Golding's translation of Ovid's *Metamorphoses*. Oberon, the fairy-king, had recently appeared in Greene's play *The Scottish History of James IV.*; Puck, under his name of Robin Goodfellow, was a roguish sprite, well known in English fairy-lore. Finally, in Montemayor's *Diana*, which Shakspere had made acquaintance with before *The Two Gentlemen of Verona* was written, occur some incidents which may have suggested the magic effects of the flower-juice laid upon the sleeping lovers' lids. Taking a little from this quarter and a little from that, Shakspere created out of such slight materials his marvellous Dream. The marriage of Duke Theseus and Hippolyta—who are classical in name only, being in reality romantic mediæval figures —surrounds the whole, as it were, with a magnificent frame. Theseus is Shakspere's early ideal of a heroic warrior and man of action. His life is one of splendid achievement and of joy; his love is a kind of happy victory, his marriage a triumph. From early morning, when his hounds—themselves heroic creatures—fill the valley with their "musical confusion," until mid-

night, when the Athenian clowns end their "very tragical mirth," with a Bergomask dance, Theseus displays his joyous energy and the graciousness of power. In contrast with him and his warrior bride, the figures of the young lovers look slight and graceful, and their love-perplexities and errors are seen to be among the minor and remediable afflictions of the world. Shakspere was not interested in making much distinction of character between Demetrius and Lysander, they are little more than a first lover and a second lover. Nor is Helena distinguishable from Hermia by much else than that in person she is the taller of the two and the gentler in disposition. Where there are so many contrasts, the play can admit, and perhaps needs, some uniformities. The mirth of the lovers' part of *A Midsummer Night's Dream* turns chiefly upon incidents, and therefore, as with the brothers Antipholus in *The Comedy of Errors*, differences of character are not made prominent. Here, as in the *Errors*, there are entanglements and cross-purposes. The one play has indeed been named "the mistakes of a day," and the other "the mistakes of a night:" but the difference lies deeper than such names intimate; for in the *Errors* the confusion is external to the mind, here it is internal; in the *Errors* the feelings of the actors remain constant, but the persons towards whom they are directed take the place, unobserved, one of another; here the persons remain constant, but their feelings of love, indifference, or dislike are at the mercy of mischief-making accident. It may be noticed that in *The Comedy of Errors* there is a passage (Act II. Sc. ii. L. 190–204) which looks as if when Shakspere wrote it he were already thinking of his fairy-world in *A Midsummer Night's Dream*, of the pranks of Robin Goodfellow, and of Bottom's transformation to an ass.

As the two extremes of exquisite delicacy, of dainty elegance, and, on the other hand, of thick-witted grossness and clumsiness, stand the fairy tribe and the group of Athenian handicraftsmen. The world of the poet's dream includes the two—a Titania, and a Bottom the weaver—and can bring them into grotesque conjunction. No such fairy poetry existed anywhere in English literature before Shakspere. The tiny elves, to whom a cowslip is tall, for whom the third part of a minute is an important division of time, have a miniature perfection which is charming. They delight in all beautiful and dainty things, and war with things that creep and things that fly, if they be uncomely; their lives are gay with fine frolic and delicate revelry. Puck, the jester of Fairyland, stands apart from the rest, the recognisable "lob of spirits," a rough, "fawn-faced, shock-pated little fellow, a very Shetlander among the gossamer-winged, dainty-limbed shapes around him."

The rehearsing of their play and its performance before the Duke affords a happy occasion for grouping together the carpenter, the tinker, the bellows-mender, and their fellows who have turned actors for the nonce. Bottom, in his broad-blown self-importance, his all but impenetrable self-satisfaction, stands a head and shoulders higher in absurdity than any other comic personage in Shakspere's early plays. He is the admitted king of his company, the cock of his walk—and he has a consciousness that his gifts are more than equal to his opportunities. When the ass's head is on his shoulders it seems hardly a disguise, so naturally does the human-asinine seem to come to Bottom; he might have been for twelve months Titania's long-eared love, so easily do his new honours sit upon him; nor is he more embarrassed in offering to Duke Theseus his explanations of the play. This comedy of the Athenian handicraftsmen, it should be noted, is an indirect answer to any objections which might be brought against Shakspere's attempt to represent the fairy-world, and the world of classical romance, which could be so ill set visibly before the spectators of an Elizabethan theatre. In *Pyramus and Thisbe*, an actual man with a lantern stands for the moon; another represents Wall with plaster on his fingers. Bottom and his crew assume that the spectators of a drama have no imaginations; Shakspere in his fairy *Dream* assumes that they can imagine as poetically real anything beautiful or grotesque which the poet suggests to them.

It has been conjectured that *A Midsummer Night's Dream* was written to grace the wedding of some noble person—Southampton, who was married in 1598, or Essex, who was married in 1590. But these dates are, the one too late, the other too early. The lines (Act V. Sc. i. L. 52–53)

> The thrice three Muses mourning for the death
> Of Learning, late deceased in beggary,

have been thought to refer to Robert Greene's miserable death (1592); it is much more likely, if they contain an allusion to anything contemporary, that the reference is to Spenser's poem *The Tears of the Muses* (1591). A passage (Act II. Sc. i. L. 88–118) in which Titania describes the recent ill seasons, wintry summers, flood and fog, would very aptly correspond with the disastrous years 1593 and 1594. Perhaps we may incline towards 1594 as the date of the play. It contains a large proportion of rhyming lines; but the character of the play naturally calls for this. Such a succession of rhymes repeating a single sound, as occur in Act III. Sc. i. L. 168–177, and Act IV. Sc. i. L. 90–97, evidently are introduced with a special purpose. The play has the gaiety, the fancifulness, and the want of either deep thought or passion which we might expect in an early drama.

It was probably acted before Elizabeth. The praise of "single blessedness" (Act I. Sc. i. L. 74–78) may have been designed to please the ears of the maiden queen; and Oberon's vision (Act II. Sc. i. L. 148–168) contains a splendid piece of poetical homage to her. The "fair vestal throned by the west," is certainly

Elizabeth. It was supposed by Warburton that by "the mermaid on a dolphin's back" was meant Mary Queen of Scots (the *dauphin's* wife), and by the "stars," the English nobles who fell in her quarrel. It has been shown, however, that a mermaid on a dolphin's back, and shooting fires, actually formed part of the Kenilworth festivities with which Leicester entertained Elizabeth, when aiming at his mistress' hand, and which Shakspere as a boy may have witnessed. Elizabeth escaped heart-whole, but Lettice, wife of the Earl of Essex, was at that time falsely loved by Leicester, and she it has been suggested—perhaps over-ingeniously—may be "the little western flower."

The action of the play is comprised within three days, ending at twelve o'clock on the night of May-day. The notes of time given in the opening lines of the play are inconsistent with this statement, but the inconsistency is Shakspere's own.

Two quarto editions, of which the second was probably pirated, were issued in the year 1600.

7. **King Henry VI., Parts II. and III.**, are recasts of two older plays—*The First Part of the Contention*, &c. (published 1594), and *The True Tragedie of Richard Duke of Yorke*, &c. (published 1595). About 3241 lines of these old plays reappear either in the same or in an altered form in 2 and 3 *Henry VI.*, what remains, nearly one-half of the *Henry VI.* (2736 lines) being altogether new. No question in Shakspere scholarship is more perplexing and difficult than that of the authorship of these four connected historical dramas.

It is impossible here to enter into this discussion, but the chief rival theories must be briefly stated:

(1) Shakspere was author of the four plays: the opinion of Knight, and almost certainly erroneous.

(2) Greene and Peele were the authors of the old plays; Shakspere the reviser, retaining portions

of his predecessor's work, altering portions, and adding passages of his own.—(MALONE.)

(3) Marlowe, Greene, Shakspere (and perhaps Peele), were the authors of the old plays; Shakspere alone the reviser, and the portions common to the old plays, and 2 and 3 *Henry VI.* were Shakspere's contributions to the original dramas, which he now reclaimed for his own use.—(R. GRANT WHITE.)

(4) Marlowe and Greene (and possibly Peele) the authors of the old plays; Shakspere and Marlowe the revisers, working as collaborateurs.—(MISS JANE LEE.)

The third and fourth of these theories may be said to have driven the first and second off the field; and it will be seen that the two questions in dispute are the following: Had Shakspere a hand in the old plays? and, Had Marlowe a hand not only in the old plays, but also as reviser in the new?

Marlowe's hand is certainly visible in both the old plays and in some of the passages which appear for the first time in *Henry VI.* (see, for a striking example, 2 *Henry VI.*, Act IV. Sc. i. L. 1–11). Shakspere and the "Dead Shepherd" whom he alludes to in *As You Like It*, were then fellow-workers, and if rivals, their rivalry was noble. But in truth, at this time Marlowe, by virtue of his prestige, and because he had found his proper genius while Shakspere was still feeling after his true direction, would be the superior, and the degree of independence of spirit shown in Shakspere's work, although he is under the influence of Marlowe, is interesting and remarkable. It is not easy to attribute the humorous Jack Cade scenes in *The First Part of the Contention* to any other writer than Shakspere; if he be excluded from a share in that play, they must be ascribed to Greene. "Speaking broadly," writes Miss Lee, "in *The Contention* and *True Tragedie* the characters of King Henry VI., Cardinal Beaufort, York" [but many of York's speeches, she adds, must have been written by Greene], "Suffolk, the two Cliffords" [and Richard] "are drawn by Marlowe; but I say this with the reservation, that in certain scenes written by Greene the parts of these characters were written by Greene also. . . . Turning next from Marlowe's characters to the characters of Greene—Duke Humphrey I believe to be in a measure his, and also the Duchess Eleanor, Clarence, Edward IV., . . . Elizabeth, . . . Sir John Hume" [and Jack Cade].

The following provisional division of work is made by the same critic. S. and M. stand for Shakspere and Marlowe, the revisers; *M. G.* and *P.* (in italics) stand for Marlowe, Greene, and Peele, the supposed authors of *The Contention* and *True Tragedie*. The table shows in detail how the revision was effected. Thus "Act I. Sc. i. S., *M. and G.*" means that in this scene Shakspere was revising the work of Marlowe and Greene; "Act IV. Sc. x. S. and M., *G.*" means that here Shakspere and Marlowe were revising the work of Greene.

Henry VI. Part II.—Act I. Sc. i. S., *M. and G.*; Sc. ii. S., *G.*; Sc. iii. S., *G. and M.*; Sc. iv. S., *G.* Act II. Sc. i. S., *G.*; Sc. ii. S., *M. and* (?) *G.*; Sc. iii. S. and (?) M., *G.* Sc. iv. S., *G.* Act III. Sc. i. S. and (?) M., *M. and G.*; Sc. ii. S. and M., *M. and G.*; Sc. iii. S., *M.* Act. IV. Sc. i. M., *G.*; Sc. ii., iii., iv. S., *G.*; Sc. v. unrevised, *G.*; Sc. vi., vii., viii., ix. S., *G.*; Sc. x. S. and M., *G.* Act V. Sc. i. M. and S., *M. and* (?) *G.*; Sc. ii. M. and S., *G. and M.*; Sc. iii. S., *G. and M.*

Henry VI. Part III.—Act I. Sc. i. S., *M.*; Sc. ii. M., *M.*; Sc. iii. unrevised, *M.*; Sc. iv. S., *M. and* (?) *G.* Act II. Sc. i. M. and (?) S., *M. and* (?) *G.*; Sc. ii. (?) M., *M. G. and* (?) *P.*; Sc. iii. S. and M., *M.*; Sc. iv. M., *G.*; Sc. v. S. and (?) M., *G.*; Sc. vi. M., *M. and G.* Act III. Sc. i. S., *G.*; Sc. ii. S., *G. and* (?) *M.*; Sc. iii. (?) M., *G. and* (?) *P.* Act IV. Sc. i. S., *G.*; Sc. ii. M., *M.*; Sc. iii. S., *M.*; Sc. iv. S., *G.*; Sc. v. S. (?) *G.*; Sc. vi., vii. S., *G.*; Sc. viii. S., (?) Act v. Sc. i. M. *G. and* (?) *P.*; Sc. ii. S., *M. and G.*; Sc. iii. M., *G.*; Sc. iv. S., *G. and* (?) *P.*; Sc. v., vi. S., *M.*; Sc. vii. unrevised, *G.*

"The *Third Part of Henry VI.* underwent a much less thorough revision than the second. Out of 3075 lines in Part II. there are 1715 new lines, some 840 altered lines (many but very slightly altered), and some 520 old lines. In Part III., out of 2902 lines, there are about 1021 new lines, about 871 altered lines, and about 1010 old lines. Hence it is that in Part III.

there are fewer resemblances of thought and verbal expression to Shakspere's undoubted writings than in Part II."—(MISS LEE.)

In connection with this subject the passage in *Greenes Groatsworth of Wit* (see p. 21) should be remembered, in which he speaks with virulent hatred of Shakspere, and tries to incite Marlowe to a like hatred, parodying in the same passage a line which appears in the *True Tragedie*, and which is transferred from it to 3 *Henry VI*.

Shakspere could perhaps have had, as a young writer, no better training for the work of dramatist than the going over, with such a master as Marlowe, the work of Marlowe himself and of other distinguished dramatists. It is evident that already in variety of imagination and sound judgment Shakspere is superior to his great contemporary. From working on these plays Shakspere got the motive and impulse to carry on the story in his own wonderful *Richard III.*, and was thus engaged in a dramatic study of English history which he pursued until at length his latest historical play (except *Henry VIII.*) met his earliest work, and the heroic ruler, Henry V., expressing Shakspere's adult patriotism and political feeling, stood hard by his earliest English king, Henry VI., the weak and unhappy child of that heroic monarch.

Three subjects in the main make up the *Second Part of Henry VI.*: the quarrels of the nobles, leading to the fall and murder of the king's uncle Gloster; the unrighteous passion of the Queen—the terrible Margaret of Anjou and her lover, Suffolk, with Suffolk's murder by pirates; and last, the unsuccessful insurrection of Cade. There is noble material for tragic poetry here, and it is treated in some portions in a masterly way. The Third Part deals with the varying fortunes of the civil war. The chief personal force upon the side of Lancaster resides in Queen Margaret; the great Duke of York dies; but his place is filled by the portentous figure of Richard, so terrible by his energy, his disregard of moral restraint, and his remorseless hatred of those who are opposed to him. Henry is the feeblest of Shakspere's English kings: possessed of that negative kind of saintliness which shuns evil, but shunning courageous effort also, he becomes the cause or occasion of almost as much evil as if he were actively a criminal.

When the revision of the old plays was made we cannot be certain, perhaps a short time before Marlowe's death, in 1593, perhaps at a date previous to Greene's sneering allusion to Shakspere in the *Groatsworth of Wit*, 1592.

[See on this play Malone's essay, *Variorum Shakspere*, 1821, vol. xviii.; Knight's essay in his *Pictorial Shakspere*; Mr. R. Grant White's essay in his edition of Shakespeare, vol. vii.; and that of Miss Lee in the *Transactions of the New Shakspere Society*, 1876.]

8. **King Richard III.**, because, among other alleged reasons, it exhibits so much smaller a proportion of rhyme than *King Richard II.*, is held by some critics to be the later of the two in the chronological order; but here Shakspere was working, though not in the presence, yet under the influence and in the manner of the great master of dramatic blank verse, Marlowe. *Richard III.* carries on with the highest energy, and we may suppose, after brief delay on Shakspere's part, the subject of the fortunes of the house of York from the point where it was dropped in 3 *Henry VI.* It would hardly be possible that Shakspere should subsequently continue to write in a manner so Marlowesque as that of *Richard III.*; he was not yet in comedy or tragedy delivered from rhyme. What more natural than that he should pass in *Richard II.* to a manner, perhaps inferior in some respects, but more his own, more varied, more subtle, and marked by finer, if less forcible characterisation? *King Richard III.* can hardly be later in date than 1593.

Shakspere was indebted little, if at all, to the old play *The True Tragedie of Richard III.*, and certainly not at all to Dr. Legge's Latin play upon the same subject. A highly popular subject with Elizabethan audiences this was—the fall of the Yorkist usurper, and the accession of the first Tudor king as champion of justice. Shakspere's play was printed in quarto in seven editions between 1597 and 1630. His materials the dramatist found in Holinshed and Hall. Holinshed's account gives two views of Richard's character; one, in the portion of history previous to the death of Edward IV., in which Richard is painted in colours not so deeply, so diabolically black; and the second, in which he appears as he does in Shakspere's play. This second and darker representation of Richard was derived by Holinshed from Sir T. More's *History of Edward V. and Richard III.*, and More had himself probably derived it from Cardinal Morton, chancellor of Henry VII. and the enemy of Richard.

The entire play may be said to be the exhibition of the one central character of Richard; all subordinate persons are created that he may wreak his will upon them. This is quite in the manner of Marlowe. Like Marlowe also is the fierce energy of the central character, untempered by moral restraints, the heaping up of violent deeds, the absence of all reserve or mystery in the characterisation, the broad and bold touches, the demoniac force and intensity of the whole. There is something sublime and terrible in so great and fierce a human energy as that of Richard, concentrated within one withered and distorted body. This is the evil offspring and flower of the long and cruel civil wars—this distorted creature, a hater and scorner of man, an absolute cynic, loveless and alone, disregarding all human bonds and human affections, yet full of intellect, of fire, of power. The figure of Queen Margaret, prophesying destruction to her adversaries, and bitterly rejoicing in the fulfilment of her prophecies, is introduced without historical warrant, but in a manner most impressive. The accumulated crimes of civil war are at last atoned for, and the evil which culminates in Richard falls with Richard from its bad eminence. The loveless solitude, haunted by terrible visions of his victims, on the night before his last battle, almost overmasters his resolution; but the stir and movement of the morning reanimates him, and he dies in a paroxysm of the rage of battle. Richmond conquers as the representative of the cause of God.

The Folio (1623) text of this play differs in many small points, and in some important particulars, from that of the Quartos which all follow the first Quarto, 1597. Whether the Folio gives the text as corrected by Shakspere himself, or as altered by an inferior hand from a copy previously corrected and augmented by Shakspere, is a question in dispute. (See *New Shakspere Society's Transactions*, 1875-76.)

9. **Venus and Adonis** was entered in the Stationers' Company register on April 18, 1593, and was published the same year. The poem at once became popular, and before the close of 1602 it had been reprinted no fewer than six times. "As the soule of Euphorbus," wrote Meres in his *Wit's Treasury* (1598), "was thought to live in Pythagoras, so the sweete wittie soule of Ovid lives in mellifluous and hony-tongued Shakespeare; witnes his *Venus and Adonis*, his *Lucrece*, his sugred Sonnets among his private friends, &c." Ovid had told the story of the love of Venus for Adonis, and the death of the beautiful hunter by a wild boar's tusk: the coldness of Adonis, his boyish disdain of love, was an invention of later times; and it is in this later form that Shakspere imagines the subject. The *Metamorphoses* of Ovid had been translated into English verse by Arthur Golding (1567), and Shakspere, if not now, was certainly at a later date acquainted with this translation. A speech of Prospero in *The Tempest* (Act V. Sc. i.), beginning—

Ye elves of hills, brooks, standing lakes, and groves,

is suggested by a passage of Golding's Ovid; but

Shakspere's treatment of the subject of the *Venus and Adonis* has less in common with Ovid than with a short poem by a contemporary writer of sonnets and lyrical poems, Henry Constable, which appeared in a collection of verse published in 1600, under the name of *England's Helicon*. It is uncertain which of the two poems, Constable's or Shakspere's, was the earlier written.

When *Venus and Adonis* appeared Shakspere was twenty-nine years of age; the Earl of Southampton, to whom it was dedicated, was not yet twenty. In the dedication the poet speaks of these "unpolisht lines" as "the first heire of my invention." Did Shakspere mean by this that *Venus and Adonis* was written before any of his plays, or before any plays that were strictly original—his own "invention?" or does he, setting plays altogether apart, which were not looked upon as literature, in a high sense of the word, call it his first poem because he had written no earlier narrative or lyrical verse? We cannot be sure. It is possible, but not likely, that he may have written this poem before he left Stratford, and have brought it up with him to London. More probably it was written in London, and perhaps not long before its publication. The year 1593, in which the poem appeared, was a year of plague; the London theatres were closed: it may be that Shakspere, idle in London, or having returned for a while to Stratford, then wrote the poem. Whenever written, it was elaborated with peculiar care. The subject of the poem is sensual, but with Shakspere it becomes rather a study or analysis of passion and the objects of passion, than in itself passionate. Without being dramatic, the poem contains the materials for dramatic poetry, set forth at large. The descriptions of English landscape and country life are numerous, and give a spirit of breezy life and health to portions of the poem which could ill afford to lose anything that is fresh and healthful.

10. **Lucrece** was entered in the Stationers' register May 9, 1594, and was published the same year. Like the *Venus and Adonis*, it is dedicated to the Earl of Southampton, having been perhaps the "graver labour" promised in the dedication of the *Venus and Adonis*. The two poems resemble one another in several respects, especially in the detailed descriptive style, which draws out at length the particulars of a scene, an incident, or an emotion. The poem of later date, however, exhibits far less immaturity than does the "first heire" of Shakspere's invention. Part of this may be due to the fact that the subject is deeper and more passionate: instead of the enamoured Venus we have here the pure and noble Lucretia; instead of the boy Adonis, the powerful figure of the evil Tarquin. The versification is freer and bolder; in the *Venus and Adonis* the stanza was one of six lines, consisting of a rhymed quatrain followed by a couplet; here a fifth line is introduced between the quatrain and couplet, rhyming with lines two and four. This structure tends to encourage more variety in the arrangement of pauses, and may perhaps, in some degree, explain the fact that run-on lines are much more frequent in the *Lucrece* than in the *Venus and Adonis*. The proportion of the run-on lines in the *Lucrece* is 1 in 10·81, in *Venus and Adonis* 1 in 25·40. (FURNIVALL.) The *Lucrece* was a poem highly admired by Shakspere's contemporaries, and was several times republished, though less often than the *Venus*. The story of Lucretia is told by Livy and Ovid, and was versified by Gower, and again related in Paynter's *Palace of Pleasure*, 1567.

11. **Romeo and Juliet.**—The story of the unhappy lovers of Verona, as a supposed historical occurrence, is referred to the year 1303; but no account of it exists of an earlier date than that of Luigi da Porto, about 1530. A tale in some respects similar is set forth in the *Ephesiaca* of Xenophon of Ephesus, a mediæval Greek romance writer; and one essentially the same,

narrating the adventures of Mariotto and Gianozza of Siena, is found in a collection of tales by Masuccio of Salerno, 1476; but Da Porto first names Romeo and Giulietta, and makes them children of the rival Veronese houses. The story quickly acquired an European celebrity. Altering the name and some particulars, Adrian Sevin relates it (about 1542) for his French patroness; Gherardo Boldiero turns it into verse for his readers at Venice. Bandello, partly recasting the narrative, recounts it once more in his Italian collection of novels, 1554; and five years later Pierre Boisteau, probably assisted by Belleforest, translates Bandello's Italian into French, and again recasts the story (1559). In three years more it touches English soil. Arthur Brooke in 1562 produced his long metrical version, founded upon Boisteau's novel, and a prose translation of Boisteau's *Histoire de Deux Amans*, appeared in Paynter's *Palace of Pleasure*, 1567. We have here reached Shakspere's sources: Paynter he probably consulted; in nearly all essentials he follows the *Romeus and Juliet* of Brooke. It must be noted, however, that Brooke speaks of having seen "the same argument lately set forth on stage"— probably the English stage; it is therefore possible that Shakspere may have had before him an old English tragedy of *Romeo and Juliet*, of which no fragment remains with us. Resemblances between passages of Shakspere's tragedy and passages of Groto's Italian tragedy of *Hadriana* are probably due to accident.

The precise date of Shakspere's play is uncertain. In 1597 it was published in quarto, "as it hath been often (with great applause) plaid publiquely by the right Honourable the L.[ord] of Hunsdon his servants." Now the Lord Chamberlain, Henry Lord Hunsdon, died July 22, 1596; his son, George Lord Hunsdon, was appointed Chamberlain in April, 1597. Before July, 1596, or after April, 1597, the theatrical company would have been styled by the more honourable designation, "the Lord Chamberlain's servants;" but during the interval they would be described as on the title-page of the quarto. The Nurse's mention of the earthquake (Act I. Sc. iii. L. 23), "'Tis since the earthquake now eleven years," has been referred to as giving the date, 1591, a memorable earthquake, felt in London, having occurred eleven years previously, in 1580; but, while professing an infallibly accurate recollection, the garrulous old woman blunders sadly about her dates, so that even if an actual English earthquake were alluded to, the point of the jest may have been in the inaccuracy of the reference. Several lines in Romeo's speech in presence of Juliet in the tomb (Act V. Sc. iii. L. 74–120) seem written with a haunting recollection of passages in Daniel's *Complainte of Rosamunde* (1592). The internal evidence favours the opinion that this tragedy was an early work of the poet, and that it was subsequently revised and enlarged. There is much rhyme, and much of this is in the form of alternate rhyme; the forced playing upon words, and the overstrained conceits (see, for example, Act I. Sc. iii. 81–92) point to an early date. If, however, rhymed verse be present in large quantity, the quality of the scenes chiefly written in blank verse is far higher than that of the rhyming passages. We may perhaps accept the opinion that *Romeo and Juliet* was begun, and in part written, as early as 1591, and that it assumed its final form about 1597. The first quarto, already mentioned (1597), is a pirated edition, "made up partly from copies of portions of the original play, partly from recollection and from notes taken during the performance." The second quarto, 1599, is described on the title-page as "newly-corrected, augmented, and amended." This perhaps exaggerates the fact; but here we obtain a true representation of the play, and comparing this with the earlier text, it appears that the play "underwent revision, received some slight augmentation, and in some few places must have been entirely rewritten."

Romeo and Juliet, apart from its intrinsic beauty,

is of deep interest when viewed as Shakspere's first tragedy, and as a work which probably occupied his thoughts, from time to time, during a series of years. It is a young man's tragedy, in which Youth and Love are brought face to face with Hatred and Death. There are some lines in *A Midsummer Night's Dream* in which the poet compares "the course of true love" to that of lightning in midnight.

> And ere a man hath power to say, Behold,
> The jaws of darkness do devour it up:
> So quick bright things come to confusion.

It is thus that love is conceived in *Romeo and Juliet* —it is sudden, it is intensely bright for a moment, and then it is swallowed up in darkness. The action is accelerated by Shakspere to the utmost, the four or five months of Brooke's poem being reduced to as many days. On Sunday the lovers meet, next day they are made one in marriage, on Tuesday morning at dawn they part, and they are finally reunited in the tomb on the night of Thursday. Shakspere does not close the tragedy with Juliet's death: as he has shown in the first scene the hatred of the houses through the comic quarrel of the servants, thereby introducing the causes which produce the tragic issue, so in the last scene he shows us the houses sorrowfully reconciled over the dead bodies of a son and a daughter.

Romeo's nature is prone to enthusiastic feeling, and, as it were, vaguely trembling in the direction of love before he sees Juliet; to meet her gives form and fixity to his vague emotion. Shakspere, following Brooke's poem, has introduced Romeo as yielding himself to a fanciful, boy's love of the disdainful beauty, Rosaline; and some of the love-conceits and love-hyperbole of the first act are intended as the conventional amorous dialect of the period. To Juliet—a girl of fourteen—love comes as a thing previously unknown; it is at once terrible and blissful (see Act II. Sc. ii. L. 116-120); she rises, through love, and sorrow, and trial, from a child into a heroic woman.

After Shakspere has exalted their enthusiastic joy and rapture to the highest point, he suddenly casts it down. Romeo is at first completely unmanned; but Juliet exhibits a noble fortitude and self-command. The scene of the parting of husband and wife at dawn is a fitting pendant to the scene in the moonlit garden, where the confession of their love is made; the one scene wrought out of divinely-mingled love and joy, the other of divinely-mingled love and sorrow. When Romeo leaves his young wife, the marriage with Paris is pressed upon her by the hot-tempered old Capulet, by her mother, and by her gross-hearted Nurse. Juliet is henceforth in a solitude almost as deep as that of her tomb. The circumstance of bringing Paris across Romeo in the churchyard, with his death before the tomb, is of Shakspere's invention. Paris comes strewing flowers for the lost Juliet—Romeo comes to find her and to die. Paris scatters his blossoms with one of those graceful love-speeches, in the form of a rhymed sextet, which flowed from Romeo's lips in Act I.—Romeo's speech is in earnest and plain blank verse, for he has now dropped all unrealities and prettinesses. In Luigi da Porto, in Bandello, and in a modern version of Shakspere's play by Garrick, Juliet awakes from her sleep while Romeo still lives; Shakspere's treatment of this scene as to this particular is the same as that of Brooke and Paynter.

Mercutio and the Nurse are almost creations of Shakspere. Brooke had described Mercutio as "a lion among maidens," and speaks of his "ice-cold hand;" but it was the dramatist who drew at full-length the figure of this brilliant being, who though with wit running beyond what is becoming, and effervescent animal spirits, yet acts as a guardian of Romeo, and is always a gallant gentleman. He dies forcing a jest through his bodily anguish, but he dies on Romeo's behalf: the scene darkens as his figure disappears. The Nurse is a coarse, kindly, garrulous, consequential old body, with vulgar feelings, and a vulgarised air of rank; she is on terms of longstanding familiarity with her master, her mistress, and Juliet, and takes all manner of liberties with them; but love has made Juliet a woman, and independent of her old foster-mother. Friar Laurence, gathering his simples and moralising to himself, is a centre of tranquillity in the midst of turmoil and passion; but it may be doubted that his counsels of moderation, and amiable scheming to reconcile the houses through Romeo's marriage with Juliet, contain more real wisdom than do the passionate dictates of the lovers' hearts.

The scene is essentially Italian: the burning noons of July in the Italian city inflame the blood of the street quarrellers; the voluptuous moonlit nights are only like a softer day. And the characters are Italian, with their lyrical ardour, their southern impetuosity of passion, and the southern forms and colour of their speech.

12. **King Richard II.** appeared in quarto, 1597. In 1608 a third edition was published "With new additions of the Parliament Scene and the deposing of King Richard," that is to say, with the added lines 154–318 in Act IV. Sc. i. It is probable that these lines were written as part of the original play, but relating as they did to the deposition of a king, had been omitted for fear of giving offence at a time when the Pope and Catholic princes were exhorting her subjects to dethrone Elizabeth. Line 321—

> A woeful pageant have we here beheld—

which is found in the first quarto, seems to refer to the deposition. A play upon this subject was actually used for a political purpose in the year 1601, having been played on the afternoon before the revolt of Essex, by order of Sir Gilly Merrick, an adherent of the Earl. That this was Shakspere's play is very unlikely. Another *Richard II.* was seen at the Globe Theatre, 1611, by Dr. Simon Forman, but neither was it—as Forman's description of it makes evident—the play of Shakspere. The date of *Richard II.* is not ascertained, but it has been assigned, with an appearance of probability, to the year 1593 or 1594. Whether it preceded or followed *Richard III.* is a question in dispute. It is the inferior scenes in this play which contain most rhymed verse; the dramatist exhibits, as in *Romeo and Juliet*, mastery over blank verse, but is not yet free from the tendency to fall back into rhyme. Upon the whole, *Richard II.* bears closer affinity to *King John* than to any other of Shakspere's plays. Marlowe's genius, however, still exercises an influence over Shakspere, the *Edward II.* of the earlier poet haunting Shakspere's imagination while he was fashioning his *Richard II.*

Having in *Richard III.* (if, as I believe, it preceded the present play) brought the civil wars of England to an issue and an end, Shakspere turned back to the reign of the earlier Richard, whose deposition led the way to the disputed succession and the conflicts of half a century later. The interest of the play centres in two connected things—the personal contrast between the falling and the rising kings, and the political action of each; the misgovernment of the one inviting and almost justifying the usurpation of the other. At the outset, Shakspere fixes the attention upon the murder of the King's uncle, the Duke of Gloucester, who was said by Mowbray to have died in his custody at Calais, but who was not unreasonably believed to have been put to death by Richard's order. Bolingbroke in striking at Mowbray was striking at Richard, and a dark deed of violence is brought into notice as the starting-point of the events which led to Richard's fall. But he has not only done violence to one of his own house, he has wronged the people of England. His upstart favourites, his blank charters, his farming of the realm, are so many blows pointed at the life of his country, and, as has been observed, the national aspect of the quarrel is brought forward by Hereford's proud assertion of his nationality, and by Gaunt's magnificent eulogy of England. But Shakspere—although no zealot on behalf of the divine right of kings—does not applaud usurpation as the means of destroying a tyranny; from the Bishop of Carlisle's lips proceeds a prophecy of the future horrors of civil war which must ensue from the violent dethronement of the king.

Richard, although possessed of a certain regal charm, and power of attaching tender natures to himself, is deficient in all that is sterling and real in manhood. He is self-indulgent, has much superficial sensitiveness, loves to contemplate, in a romantic way, whatever is pathetic or passionate in life, possesses a kind of rhetorical imagination, and has abundant command of delicate and gleaming words. His will is nerveless, he is incapable of consistency of feeling, incapable of strenuous action. Bolingbroke, on the other hand, who pushes Richard from the throne, is a man framed for such material success as waits on personal ambition. He is not, like his son Henry V., filled with high enthusiasm and sacred force derived from the powers of heaven and of earth. All Bolingbroke's strength and craft are his own. His is a resolute gaze which sees his object far off, and he has persistency and energy of will to carry him forward without faltering. He is not cruel, but shrinks from no deed that is needful to his purpose because the deed is cruel. His faculties are strong and well-knit. There is no finer contrast in Shakspere's historical plays than that between the figures of the formidable king of deeds, and the romantic king of hectic feelings and brilliant words.

Coincidences have been pointed out between *Richard II.* and Daniel's *Civil Wars*, 2nd edition, 1595: if either borrowed from the other, the borrower was probably Daniel.

13. **King John** departs farther from the facts of

history than any other of Shakspere's historical plays. He here follows for the most part not Holinshed, but an old play in two parts, which appeared in 1591, entitled *The Troublesome Raigne of King John of England*. He follows it, however, not in the close way in which he had previously worked when writing 2 and 3 *Henry VI.*; the main incidents are the same, but Shakspere elevates and almost recreates the characters; for the most eloquent and poetical passages no original is to be found in the old play. The character of the king grows more darkly treacherous in Shakspere's hands: barely a hint of the earlier author suggested the scene, so powerful and so subtle, in which John insinuates to Hubert his murderous desires; the boyish innocence of Arthur, and the pathos of his life, become real and living as they are dealt with by the imagination of Shakspere; Constance is no longer a fierce and ambitious virago, but a passionate sorrowing mother; Faulconbridge is ennobled by a manly tenderness and a purer patriotism. Shakspere depicts, with true English spirit, the ambition, the political greed, the faithlessness, the sophistry of the court of Rome; but he wholly omits a ribald scene of the old play, in which the licentiousness of monasteries is exposed to ridicule.

As to the date of *King John*, all we can assert with confidence is that it lies somewhere between the early histories *Henry VI., Parts I., II.,* and *III.,* with *Richard III.,* and the group of later histories, the trilogy consisting of 1 and 2 *Henry IV.* and *Henry V.* Thus in the historical series it is brought close to *Richard II.* Neither play contains prose, but the treatment of Faulconbridge's part shows more approach to the alliance of a humorous or comic element with history (which becomes complete in *Henry IV.*) than does anything in the play of *Richard II. King John* and *Richard II.* have the common characteristic of containing very inferior dramatic work side by side with work of a high and difficult kind. The chief point of difference with respect to form is that *Richard II.* contains a much larger proportion of rhymed verse, and on the whole we shall perhaps not err in regarding *Richard II.* as the earlier of the two.

Magna Charta, and the struggle of the nobles in England for their rights and those of the people, do not attract Shakspere away from what is more susceptible of dramatic treatment—the deeds and the passions of individual actors in history. A mother's grief for her lost boy seems to him a more poetical theme than regulations respecting aids and scutages. It is the shame and weakness of the reign of the royal malefactor, John—himself represented as a weak and dastardly usurper—rather than what makes it politically illustrious, on which Shakspere dwells. A strong breath of patriotism, nevertheless, breathes through the play, and this fills and buoys up, amid all disasters, the spirit of Cœur de Lion's bastard son. The play contains three large and splendidly-drawn figures: the king, basest of all kings of England in Shakspere's eyes, no strong malefactor, like *Richard III.*, but capable of all treason, and of every degrading submission; Constance, who is the embodiment of a mother's violent passions of love and grief, yet weak with the weakness of her sex; and Faulconbridge, the typical Englishman, with his courage, his tenderness, his frankness, his contempt for unreality and affectation, his national pride. Among these and the other forces of the play, Arthur moves with a pathetic beauty, gentleness, and innocence, as a lamb among wolves and lions.

14. **The Merchant of Venice** we place by itself, midway between the group of Shakspere's early comedies and that more brilliant group of comedies which clusters about the year 1600. With the early comedies it is allied by the frequent rhymes, the occasional doggerel verse, and the numerous classical allusions. Launcelot and Nerissa resemble Launce and Lucetta of *The Two Gentlemen of Verona*; and the scene (Act I. Sc. ii) in

which the waiting-maid names in succession Portia's lovers, for her mistress to pass her lively criticism upon them, is almost a reproduction of the scene (Act I. Sc. ii.) of *The Two Gentlemen*, where Julia and Lucetta hold a similar dialogue. It may be noted, however, that while the earlier treatment of this incident is in verse, for the most part rhymed, the later is in prose; the parts assigned to maid and mistress are transposed —in the earlier play it is the maid who is the critic; and while Lucetta dismisses the lovers with a brief comment on the personality of each, Portia makes each lover the occasion for a vivacious piece of satire on the peculiarities of the nation to which he belongs. Thus Shakspere could work out his ideas a second time without precisely repeating himself. With the later group of comedies *The Merchant of Venice* stands connected by its centring the interest of the drama in the development of character, and by the variety, depth, and beauty of the characterisation. No person depicted in any preceding comedy can compare in vigour of drawing and depth of colour with Shylock; and Portia is the first of Shakspere's women who unites in beautiful proportion, intellectual power, high and refined, with unrestrained ardour of the heart.

The story of the caskets and the story of the pound of flesh had been told separately many times and in various countries. The former is first found in the mediæval Greek romance of *Barlaam and Josaphat*, by Joannes Damascenus (about A.D. 800); in another form it is told by the English poet Gower, and the Italian novelist Boccaccio. But points of resemblance are most striking between Shakspere's version of the casket incident and that given in the collection of stories so popular in the Middle Ages, the *Gesta Romanorum*. The incident of the pound of flesh also appears in the *Gesta*; it is found in a long religious poem, written in the Northumbrian dialect about the end of the thirteenth century, the *Cursor Mundi*, in an old ballad "showing the crueltie of

Gernutus a Jew," and elsewhere; there are Persian and Egyptian versions of the tale, which itself perhaps originally came from the East. The form in which we have it in Shakspere is most closely connected with the version found in a collection of tales, *Il Pecorone*, written by Ser Giovanni, a notary of Florence, about A.D. 1378. Here, and only here, the incident of the ring, which forms the subject of the fifth act of *The Merchant of Venice*, is given; and here the name Belmont appears. It is probable, however, that Shakspere to become acquainted with these stories had not to go to *Il Pecorone* and the *Gesta Romanorum*. Stephen Gosson writing in 1579, in his *Schoole of Abuse*, about plays which were "tollerable at sometime," mentions "the Jew . . . showne at the Bull . . . representing the greedinesse of worldly chusers and bloody mindes of usurers." The greediness of worldly choosers seems to point to the casket incident, and the bloody minds of usurers to that of the pound of flesh; we therefore infer that a pre-Shaksperian play existed which combined these two incidents. And it is highly probable that Shakspere's task in the case of *The Merchant of Venice*, as afterwards in that of *King Lear*, consisted in creating from old and worthless dramatic material found among the crude productions of the early English theatre, those forms of beauty and of majesty with which we are familiar.

Although the play is named after the merchant, Antonio, he is not the chief dramatic person; he forms, however, a centre around which the other characters are grouped: Bassanio, his friend; Shylock, his enemy and would-be murderer; Portia, his saviour. Antonio's part is rather a passive than an active one; he is to be an object of contention and a prize; much is to be done against him and on his behalf, but not so much is to be done *by* him; and therefore, although his character is very firmly conceived and clearly indicated, his part is subdued and kept low, lest it might interfere with the exhibition of the two chief forces of the play—the cruel masculine force of Shylock, which holds the merchant in its relentless, vice-like grip; and the feminine force of Portia, which is as bright as the sunlight, and as beneficent. Yet Shakspere is careful to interest us in Antonio, and to show us that he was worth every exertion to save. He is

> The kindest man,
> The best condition'd and unwearied spirit
> In doing courtesies, and one in whom
> The ancient Roman honour more appears
> Than any that draws breath in Italy.

When Antonio first appears he is oppressed with a sadness which he will not name to his mirthful companions. It is the sadness of having to render up his friend Bassanio to one who must henceforth take the chief place in his heart. As soon as he is left alone with his kinsman, around whom his tenderest affection has entwined itself, the merchant questions him about the lady; and Bassanio, who has known Portia already and loves her, fearing to pain his friend, dwells little on his love and much on the motives of prudence which make his marriage with a rich heiress desirable, until at the last his enthusiasm about the beauty and goodness of Portia cannot be contained. When Bassanio is setting forth for Belmont, and his friend must remain without him, Antonio wrings his hand and his eyes are filled with tears. It is the same Portia who had seemed to deprive him of friendship who afterwards gives him back not only friendship but life itself; and at Belmont, in the last act, the lovers and their friend are united in a common joy. Portia has heard her husband say that he would sacrifice " his life itself, his wife, and all the world," to save Antonio; and at Antonio's request he has parted with Portia's ring; but her playful reproaches express no jealous fear— nay, rather conceal her real joy to find the man she loves loyal to the man who had so truly loved him. The subject of friendship and love, and their mutual relations, which Shakspere had treated in *The Two*

Gentlemen of Verona, reappears, treated in a far deeper and more refined manner in the present play.

The distinction of Portia among the women of Shakspere is the union in her nature of high intellectual powers and decision of will with a heart full of ardour and of susceptibility to romantic feelings. She has herself never known trouble or sorrow, but prosperity has left her generous and quick in sympathy. Her noble use of wealth and joyous life, surrounded with flowers and fountains and marble statues and music, stands in contrast over against the hard, sad, and contracted life of Shylock, one of a persecuted tribe, absorbed in one or two narrowing and intense passions —the love of the money-bags he clutches and yet fails to keep, and his hatred of the man who had scorned his tribe, insulted his creed, and diminished his gains. Yet Shylock is not like Marlowe's Jew, Barabas, a preternatural monster. Wolf-like as his revenge shows him, we pity his joyless, solitary life; and when, ringed round in the trial scene with hostile force, he stands firm upon his foothold of the law, there is something sublime in his tenacity of passion and resolve. But we feel that it is right that this evil strength should be utterly crushed and quelled, and when Shylock leaves the court a broken man, we know it is needful that this should be so.

The choosing of the caskets shows us Portia, who will strictly interpret the law of Venice for Shylock and Antonio, loyally abiding by the provisions which her father has laid down in her own case. And Bassanio is ennobled in our eyes by his choice; for the gold, silver, and lead of the caskets, with their several inscriptions, are a test of true lovers. Bassanio does not come as a needy adventurer to choose the golden casket, or to "gain," or "get" anything, but in the true spirit of self-abandoning love "to give," not to get, "and hazard all he hath;" and having dared to give all he gains all. (See the inscriptions on the caskets.)

The lyrical boy-and-girl love of Lorenzo and Jessica brings out by contrast the grave and glad earnestness of Portia's love and Bassanio's. Jessica has not a thought of loyalty to *her* father—nor is it to be expected. The lyrical passages between Lorenzo and Jessica in the moonlit garden (Act V. Sc. i.) ending with the praise of music, contrast with Portia's generalising reflections (the wake of thought still undulating after her great intellectual effort at the trial), suggested by the light seen and music heard as she approaches her house, and by her failing to receive any pleasure from the music which Lorenzo has so eloquently praised.

The comedy must end mirthfully. After the real struggle and the strain of interest respecting Antonio's fate, we pass on to the playful differences about the rings; from the court of justice at Venice we are carried to the luminous night in the gardens of Belmont. Even Antonio's ships must not be lost; a moment of happiness after trouble cannot be too perfect.

The date of the play is uncertain. In Philip Henslowe's *Diary* mention is made, under the date August 25, 1594, of the "Venesyon comedy;" this may have been Shakspere's play, but more probably it was not. *The Merchant of Venice* is mentioned by Meres, 1598, and it was entered at Stationers' Hall in the same year, though not printed until 1600. Perhaps 1596 is as likely a date as we can fix upon. The precise year matters little if it be remembered that the play occupies an intermediate place between the early and the middle group of comedies.

15. **King Henry IV., Parts I. and II.**, may be considered as one play in ten acts. It is probable that Shakspere went on with little delay, or none, from the first part to its continuation in the second. Both were written before the entry of the first in the Stationers' register, Feb. 25, 1597–98; for the entry shows that the name of the fat knight, who originally appeared

in both parts under the name of Oldcastle, had been already altered to Falstaff. Meres makes mention of *Henry IV.*; and Ben Jonson, in *Every Man out of His Humour* (1599), alludes to Justice Silence, one of the characters of the Second Part of Shakspere's play. The materials upon which Shakspere worked in *Henry IV., Parts I.* and *II.*, and *Henry V.*, were obtained from Holinshed, and from an old play, full of vulgar mirth, and acted before 1588, *The Famous Victories of Henry V.* A Sir John Oldcastle appears in this play as one of the Prince's wild companions. That Shakspere adopted the name is evident from allusions of subsequent writers, from the circumstance that in the quarto of 1600 the name *Old* is left by mistake prefixed to a speech of Falstaff, and from Henry's punning name for the fat knight (Part I. Act I. Sc. ii. L. 48), "my old lad of the castle." Falstaff, moreover, is said to have been "page to Thomas Mowbray, Duke of Norfolk" (Part II. Act III. Sc. ii. L. 28), which the historical Oldcastle was in point of fact. This historical Oldcastle is better known as Lord Cobham, the Lollard martyr. Shakspere changed the name because he did not wish wantonly to offend the Protestant party, nor gratify the Roman Catholics (see Epilogue to Part II.). A Sir John Fastolfe had figured in the French wars of Henry VI.'s reign, and was introduced as playing a cowardly part in 1 *Henry VI.* That he also was a Lollard appears not to have been suspected, but a tradition may have lingered of his connection with a certain Boar's Head Tavern, of which Fastolfe was actually owner. By a slight modification of the name this Fastolfe of history became the more illustrious Falstaff of the dramatist's invention.

Both parts of *Henry IV.* consist of a comedy and a history fused together. The hero of the one is the royal Bolingbroke, the hero of the other is Falstaff, while Prince Henry passes to and fro between the history and the comedy, serving as the bond which unites the two. Both first and second parts, but especially the first part, were written with the utmost spirit and energy. Henry IV. is the same Bolingbroke who had been so greatly conceived in *King Richard II.*; only he is no longer in the full force of his manhood. He is worn by care and toil, harassed by the troubles of the unquiet times, yet still resolved to hold firmly what he has forcibly attained. He has tried flattery with his turbulent nobles, and he has tried to overawe them; but still they are not made loyal subjects. Scotland, Wales, the lords of the North, are in arms against him. There is a pathetic power in the figure of this weary ambitious man, who can take no rest until the rest of death comes to him.

Hotspur, who to bring him into contrast with the Prince, is made much younger than the Harry Percy of history, is as ardent in the pursuit of glory as the Prince seems to be indifferent to it. To his hot temper, and quick sense of personal honour, small matters are great; he does not see things in their true proportions; he lacks self-control, he has no easiness of nature. Yet he is gallant, chivalrous, not devoid of generosity nor of quick affections, though never in a high sense disinterested. The Prince, whom Shakspere admires and loves more than any other person in English history, afterwards to become Shakspere's ideal king of England, cares little for mere reputation. He does not think much of himself, and of his own honour; and while there is nothing to do, and his great father holds all power in his own right hand, Prince Hal escapes from the cold proprieties of the court to the boisterous life and mirth of the tavern. He is, however, only waiting for a call to action, and Shakspere declares that from the first he was conscious of his great destiny, and while seeming to scatter his force in frivolity, was holding his true self, well guarded, in reserve. May there not have been a young fellow remembered by Shakspere, who went by night on deer-stealing frolics near Stratford, who yet kept from waste and ruin a true self, with which his comrades had small acquaintance, and who now helped Shakspere to understand the nature of the wild Prince and his scapegrace adventures?

Falstaff is everything in little, or rather everything in *much*; for, is he not a tun of flesh? English literature knows no humorous creation to set beside Falstaff; and to find his equal—yet his opposite—we must turn to the gaunt figure of the romantic knight of La Mancha, in whose person Cervantes smiled away pathetically the chivalry of the Middle Ages from out our modern world. Falstaff exercises upon the reader of these plays much the same fascination which he exercised upon the Prince. We know him to be a gross-bodied, self-indulgent old sinner, devoid of moral sense and of self-respect, and yet we cannot part with him. We cannot live in this mixed world without humour, and Falstaff is humour maintaining its mastery against all antagonisms. When worsted in an encounter, then he shows himself most victorious; when escape seems least possible, then by his sleight he is in a moment most at large. We admit, however, the necessity of his utter banishment from Henry, when Henry enters upon the grave responsibilities of kingship. Still we have a tender thought for Sir John in his exile from London taverns. And at the last, when he fumbles with the sheets, and plays with flowers, when "a' went away, an it had been any christom child," we bid him adieu with a tear that does not forbid a smile.

The historical period represented by 1 *Henry IV.* dates from the battle of Holmedon Hill, Sept. 14, 1402, to the battle of Shrewsbury, July 21, 1403. 2 *Henry IV.* continues the history to the king's death and the accession of Henry V., 1413.

16. **King Henry V.** is not mentioned by Meres, and the reference in the chorus of Act V. to Essex in Ireland (see p. 35), and in the Prologue to "this wooden O," *i.e.* the Globe Theatre, built in 1599,

make it probable that 1599 was the date of its production. A pirated imperfect quarto appeared in the following year. In this play Shakspere bade farewell in trumpet tones to the history of England. It was a fitting climax to the great series of works which told of the sorrow and the glory of his country, embodying as it did the purest patriotism of the days of Elizabeth. With Agincourt and a King Henry V. we can rest content, assured that all greatness and good are possible for a loyal people; we care no longer to search the dim reports

>   Of old, unhappy, far-off things,
>   And battles long ago.

And as the noblest glories of England are presented in this play, so it presents Shakspere's ideal of active, practical, heroic manhood. If Hamlet exhibits the dangers and weakness of the contemplative nature, and Prospero, its calm and its conquest, Henry exhibits the utmost greatness which the active nature can attain. He is not an astute politician like his father: having put everything upon a sound substantial basis he need not strain anxious eyes of foresight, to discern and provide for contingencies arising out of doubtful deeds; for all that naturally comes within its range he has an unerring eye. A devotion to great objects outside of self fills him with a force of glorious enthusiasm. Hence his religious spirit and his humility or modesty—he feels that the strength he wields comes not from any clever disposition of forces due to his own prudence, but streams into him and through him from his people, his country, his cause, his God. He can be terrible to traitors, and his sternness is without a touch of personal revenge. In the midst of danger he can feel so free from petty heart-eating cares as to enjoy a piece of honest, soldierly mirth. His wooing is as plain, frank, and true as are his acts of piety. He unites around himself in loyal service the jarring nationalities of his father's time—Englishmen, Scotchmen, Welshmen, Irishmen, all are at Henry's side at Agincourt. Having presented his ideal of English kinghood, Shakspere could turn aside from history. In this play no character except Henry greatly interested Shakspere, unless it be the Welsh Fluellen, whom he loves (as Scott loved the Baron of Bradwardine) for his real simplicity underlying his apparatus of learning, and his touching faith in the theory of warfare.

17. **The Taming of the Shrew** is first found in the folio, 1623, but it is in some way closely connected with a play published in 1594, and bearing the almost identical title, *The Taming of a Shrew*. We cannot accept Pope's opinion that both plays are by Shakspere, nor agree with another critic who ingeniously maintained that the earlier printed play was the later written, being suggested by Shakspere's comedy of *the Shrew*. The play in the folio is certainly an enlargement and alteration of *The Taming of a Shrew*, and it only remains to ask, was Shakspere the sole reviser and adapter, or did his task consist of adding and altering certain scenes, so as to render yet more amusing and successful an enlarged version of the play of 1594, already made by some unknown hand? This seems upon the whole the opinion best supported by the internal evidence. In *The Taming of the Shrew* we may distinguish three parts: (1) The humorous Induction, in which Sly, the drunken tinker, is the chief person; (2) A comedy of character, the Shrew and her tamer, Petruchio, being the hero and heroine; (3) A comedy of intrigue—the story of Bianca and her rival lovers. Now the old play of *A Shrew* contains, in a rude form, the scenes of the Induction, and the chief scenes in which Petruchio and Katharina (named by the original writer Ferando and Kate) appear; but nothing in this old play corresponds with the intrigues of Bianca's disguised lovers. It is, however, in the scenes concerned with these intrigues that Shakspere's hand is least ap-

parent. It may be said that Shakspere's genius goes in and out with the person of Katharina. We would therefore conjecturally assign the intrigue-comedy,— which is founded upon Gascoigne's *Supposes*, a translation of Ariosto's *Gli Suppositi*—to the adapter of the old play, reserving for Shakspere a title to those scenes—in the main enlarged from the play of *A Shrew*—in which Katharina, Petruchio, and Grumio are speakers. Turning this statement into figures, we find that Shakspere's part of *The Taming of the Shrew* is comprised in the following portions: Induction; Act II. Sc. i. L. 169-326; Act III. Sc. ii. L. 1-125, and 151-241; Act IV. Sc. i.; Act IV. Sc. iii.; Act IV. Sc. v.; Act V. Sc. ii. L. 1-180. Such a division, it must be borne in mind, is no more than a conjecture, but it seems to be suggested and fairly indicated by the style of the several parts of the comedy.

However this may be, it is clear that Shakspere cared little for the other characters in comparison with Sly, Katharina, and Petruchio. Sly is of the family of Sancho Panza, gross and materialistic in his tastes and habits, but withal so good-humoured and self-contented that we would fain leave him unvexed by higher ideas or aspirations; all the pains taken to delude him into the notion that he is a lord will not make him essentially other than "old Sly's son, of Burton Heath," who has run up so long a score with the fat ale-wife of Wincot. The Katharina and Petruchio scenes border upon the farcical, but Shakspere's interest in the characters of the Shrew and her tamer keep these scenes from passing into downright farce. Katharina with all her indulged wilfulness and violence of temper has no evil in her; in her home-enclosure she seems a formidable creature; but when caught away by the tempest of Petruchio's masculine force, the comparative weakness of her sex shows itself; she, who has strength of her own, and has ascertained its limits, can recognise superior strength, and once subdued she is the least rebellious of subjects. Petruchio acts his assumed part "with complete presence of mind, with untired animal spirits, and without a particle of ill-humour from beginning to end." The play is full of energy and bustling movement.

Widely separated dates have been assigned for *The Taming of the Shrew*, from 1594 to 1606. The best portions are in the manner of Shakspere's comedies of the second period; and attributing the Bianca intrigue-comedy to a writer intermediate between the author of the play of *A Shrew* and Shakspere, there is no difficulty in supposing that the Shakspere scenes were written about 1597. The same spirit in which *The Merry Wives of Windsor* was created was here employed by Shakspere to furnish his theatrical company with this enlarged version of a popular comedy.

It will be noted that the comedy of *The Shrew* is a play within a play, and there is no provision, such as is found in the older *Shrew*, for disposing of Sly at the end of the fifth act. The jest of bewildering a poor man into the idea that he is rich and great is found in the *Arabian Nights*; such a jest is attributed to Philip the Good of Burgundy, and the story is given in a collection of *Tales* compiled by R. Edwards, and printed in 1570. Fletcher wrote a humorous continuation of Shakspere's play, entitled *The Woman's Prize, or Tamer Tamed*, in which Petruchio reappears.

18. **The Merry Wives of Windsor** is an offshoot from the comedy of *King Henry IV.*, while *King Henry V.* is the direct continuation of the history. Dennis, in 1702, reports a tradition that this play was written in fourteen days, by order of the Queen; and Rowe adds: "she was so well pleased with that admirable character of Falstaff, in the two parts of *Henry IV.*, that she commanded him to continue it for one play more, and to show him in love." This may have been the cause why Shakspere does not fulfil the promise made in the Epilogue of *Henry IV.*, that Falstaff should reappear with Henry V. in France; but, indeed, among the

great deeds of the victor of Agincourt there would be small room for a Falstaff. The choice of Windsor as the scene, and the compliments to the owner of Windsor Castle, and to the wearers of the Order of the Garter, suggest that the play was meant especially for the ears of Elizabeth and her courtiers. An early sketch of *The Merry Wives* was published in quarto, 1602; some touches in the play, as given in the folio, were evidently made after the accession of James I. (1603); the word "council" is altered to "king" (Act I. Sc. i. L. 113); "these knights will hack," exclaims Mrs. Page (Act II. Sc. i. L. 52), and the allusion to James's too liberal creation of knights in 1604 was probably appreciated. Some critics have held that the first sketch of *The Merry Wives* was written as early as 1592. A German duke is spoken of by Bardolph as about to visit Windsor, and his gentlemen ride off with mine host of the Garter's horses unpaid for. In the early sketch (Act IV. Sc. v. of the revised play), instead of "cousin-germans," where Evans puns upon the words *cozen* and *German*, occurs the strange "cosen garmombles." Now, Count Frederick of Mömpelgard had visited England and accompanied the Queen to Windsor, Aug. 1592; and in the passport which he received for his journey back to the Continent, we read that he shall be furnished with post-horses, and shall pay nothing for the same. Next year the Count became Duke of Wirtemberg, and in 1595 he craved that, in accordance with a promise given, Elizabeth would confer upon him the Order of the Garter, which Elizabeth, on various pretexts, declined. "Garmombles" obviously reverses the true name "Mömpelgard;" but the inference that the date of the play is 1592, because it refers to the visit of the Germans, is unwarrantable, for such an event would be remembered, and the more so because of the Duke's subsequent unavailing attempt to obtain the honour of the Garter.

If we try to make out exact relations between the characters of *The Merry Wives* and the same characters as they appear in the historical plays, we shall fail. The comedy has a certain independence of the histories, and cannot be pieced on to them in any way: the persons are the same and not the same. Mrs. Quickly, servant of Dr. Caius, has a different history from the Mrs. Quickly of the Boar's Head Tavern. At what period in Falstaff's career he pursued the Windsor wives we cannot make out for certain. Nor is he conceived in quite the same manner as the Falstaff of *Henry IV.* Here the knight is fatuous, his genius deserts him; the never-defeated hangs his head before two country dames; the buckbasket, the drench of Thames water, the blows of Ford's cudgel, are reprisals too coarse upon the most inimitable of jesters. Yet the play is indeed a merry one, with well-contrived incidents and abundance of pleasant mirth. A country air breathes over the whole, which the Gloucestershire scenes of *2 Henry IV* prepared us. "The outdoor character that the *Merry Wives* and *As You Like It* gives their tone of buoyancy and enjoyment, their rural feeling." Nowhere else has Shakspere represented English middle-class life in the country, and he has here done it with a vigorous, healthy pleasure. It is not, however, a poetical play, unless comely English maidenhood, in the person of pretty Anne Page, lend it something of poetry. There is a propriety in the fact that this comedy is written almost altogether in prose. The blunders of the French doctor and of the Welsh parson in speaking English are rather an elementary form of fun, such as may suit a somewhat rustic subject; but Sir Hugh Evans, apart from his blunders, is good company. The merry wives themselves are a delightful pair, with "their sly laughing looks, their apple-red cheeks, their brows the lines whereon look more like the work of mirth than years." And Slender, most brainless of youths, most incapable of lovers, is dear for sake of the laugh at him which pretty Anne Page must have when alone. Altogether, if we can accept Falstaff's discomfitures, it is a sunny play to laugh at if not to love.

The following sources have been pointed out as exhibiting some points of resemblance to the incidents of *The Merry Wives*, and as possibly supplying hints to Shakspere: Two tales from *Le tredici piacevoli notte*, by Straparola, and the altered version of one of these to be found in Tarlton's *Newes out of Purgatorie* (1590); the tale of Bucciolo and Pietro Paulo from the *Pecorone* of Ser Giovanni Fiorentino; finally, The Fishwife's Tale of Brainford, from *Westward for Smelts*.

19. **Much Ado about Nothing** was entered on the Stationers' register, August 23, 1600, and a well-printed quarto edition appeared in the same year. The play is not mentioned by Meres, 1598, and we may assume that it was written at some time in the interval between 1598 and 1600. For the graver portion of the play—the Claudio and Hero story—Shakspere had an original, perhaps Belleforest's translation in his *Histoires Tragiques* of Bandello's 22nd Novella. The story of Ariodante and Genevra in Ariosto's *Orlando Furioso* (canto v.) is substantially the same. This episode had been translated twice into English before Harington's complete translation of the *Orlando Furioso* appeared in 1591; and it had formed the subject of a play acted before the Queen 1582-83; the story was also told, in a somewhat altered form, by Spenser, *Faerie Queene*, ii. 4. No original has been found for the merrier portion of the play, and Benedick and Beatrice were probably creations of Shakspere. It has indeed been pointed out that at about the same date the German dramatist Jacob Ayrer, in his comedy of *The Beautiful Phœnicia*, connected the story from Bandello with a comic underplot; but the resemblances between Ayrer's comic underplot and Shakspere's loves of Beatrice and Benedick are probably accidental.

Much Ado about Nothing was popular on the stage in Shakspere's day, and has sustained its reputation. Its variety, ranging from almost burlesque to almost tragedy, and from the euphuistic speech of courtiers to the blundering verbosity of clowns, has contributed to the success of the play. The chief persons, Hero and Claudio, Beatrice and Benedick, are contrasted pairs. Hero's character is kept subdued and quiet in tone, to throw out the force and colour of the character of Beatrice; she is gentle, affectionate, tender, and if playful, playful in a gentle way. If our interest in Hero were made very strong, the pain of her unmerited shame and suffering would be too keen. And Claudio is far from being a lover like Romeo; his wooing is done by proxy, and he does not sink under the anguish of Hero's disgrace and supposed death. Don John, the villain of the piece, is a melancholy egoist, who looks sourly on all the world, and has a special grudge against his brother's young favourite Claudio. The chief love of Shakspere in the play comes out in the character of Benedick and Beatrice. They have not a jot of true misanthropy, nor of sentimentality, but are thoroughly healthy and hearty human creatures; at first a little too much self-pleased, but framed by-and-by to be highly pleased with one another. The thoughts of each from the first are preoccupied with the other, but neither will put self-esteem to the hazard of a rebuke by making the first advances in love; it only needs, however, that this danger should be removed for the pair to admit the fact that nature has made them over against one another—as their significant names suggest—for man and wife. The flouting of Benedick by Beatrice reminds us of scenes between an earlier pair of lovers, Rosaline and Berowne, in *Love's Labour's Lost*. The trick which is played upon the lovers to bring them together is one of those frauds practised upon self-love which appear in several of the comedies of this period. But neither is an egoist except in a superficial way. Beatrice is filled with generous indignation against the wrongers of her cousin, and she inspires Benedick to become (not without a touch of humorous self-consciousness) champion of the cause. Dogberry and Verges, as well as Beatrice and Benedick, are creations of Shakspere. The blundering watchmen of the time are a source of fun with several Elizabethan playwrights; but Dogberry and goodman Verges are the princes of blundering and incapable officials. It is a charming incongruity to find, while Leonato rages and Benedick offers his challenge, that the solemn ass Dogberry is the one to unravel the tangled threads of their fate. Friar Francis is a near spiritual kinsman of Friar Laurence in *Romeo and Juliet.*

20. **As You Like It** was entered on the Stationers' register together with *Henry V.*, *Much Ado about Nothing*, and Jonson's *Every Man in His Humour*, "to be staied," *i.e.* not printed; the date is August 4, but the year is not mentioned. The previous entry is dated May 27, 1600, and as the other plays were printed in 1600 and 1601, we infer that the August was that of the year 1600. The comedy is not mentioned by Meres. A line, "Who ever loved that loved not at first sight?" is quoted (Act III. Sc. v. L. 82) from Marlowe's *Hero and Leander*, which was published in 1598. We may set down the following year, 1599, as the probable date of the creation of this charming comedy.

The story is taken from Thomas Lodge's prose tale, *Rosalynde, Euphues Golden Legacie*, first printed in 1590, and a passage in Lodge's dedication probably suggested to Shakspere the name of his play. Lodge, who wrote this tale on his voyage to the Canaries, founded it in part on the Cook's Tale of Gamelyn, wrongly ascribed to Chaucer, and inserted in some editions as one of the *Canterbury Tales*. In parts of his work the dramatist follows the story-teller closely, but there are some important differences. The heroic names Orlando, Oliver, and Sir Rowland are due to

Shakspere. It was a thought of Shakspere to make the rightful and the usurping dukes, as in *The Tempest*, brothers. In Lodge's novel the girl-friends pass in the forest for lady and page, in Shakspere, for brother and sister. Shakspere omits the incident of Aliena's rescue from robbers by her future husband; love at first sight was natural in Arden, but a band of robbers would have marred the tranquillity of the scene. To Shakspere we owe the creation of the characters of Jaques, Touchstone, and Audrey.

Written perhaps immediately after *Henry V.*, the play presents a striking contrast with that high-pitched historical drama. It is as if Shakspere's imagination craved repose and refreshment after the life of courts and camps. We are still on French soil, but instead of the sound of the shock of battle at Agincourt, we hear the waving forest boughs, and the forest-streams of Arden, where "they fleet the time carelessly, as they did in the Golden World." There is an open-air feeling about this play, as there is about *The Merry Wives of Windsor*; but in *The Merry Wives* all the surroundings are English and real, here they belong to a land of romance. For the Renaissance, that age of vast energy, national enterprise, religious strife, and court intrigue, pastoral or idyllic poetry possessed a peculiar charm; the quiet and innocence of a poetical Arcadia was a solace to a life of highly-wrought ambition and aspiration.

"Sweet are the uses of adversity," moralises the banished Duke, and external, material adversity has come to him, to Rosalind, and to Orlando; but if fortune is harsh, nature—both external nature and human character—is sound and sweet, and of real suffering there is none in the play. All that is evil remains in the society which the denizens of the forest have left behind; and both seriously, in the characters of the usurping Duke and Oliver, and playfully, through Touchstone's mockery of court follies, a criticism on what is evil and artificial in society is suggested in contrast with the woodland life : yet Shakspere never falls into the conventional pastoral manner. Orlando is an ideal of youthful strength, beauty, and noble innocence of heart ; and Rosalind's bright, tender womanhood seems but to grow more exquisitely feminine in the male attire which she has assumed in self-defence. Her feelings are almost as quick and fine as those of Imogen (she has not, like Imogen, known fear and sorrow), and she uses her wit and bright play of intellect as a protection against her own eager and vivid emotions. Possessed of a delighted consciousness of power to confer happiness, she can dally with disguises, and make what is most serious to her at the same time possess the charm of an exquisite frolic.

The melancholy Jaques is charged by the Duke with having been a libertine ; he has certainly tasted all manner of experiences, but not very earnestly pursued either good or evil. He is a sentimentalist, and in some degree a superficial cynic. Yet the Duke loves his company, and at the last can ill part with him, when to try one newer experience Jaques will join the Duke's brother, who has put on a religious life. Jaques is not a bad-hearted egoist, like Don John, but he is a perfectly idle seeker for new sensations and an observer of his own feelings ; he is weary of all that he has found, and especially professes to despise the artificial society, which yet he never really escapes from, as the others do. His wisdom is half foolery, as Touchstone's foolery is half wisdom. Touchstone is the daintiest fool of the comedies, and when we compare him with the clowns of *The Comedy of Errors* or *The Two Gentlemen of Verona*, we perceive how Shakspere's humour has grown in refinement.

21. **The Passionate Pilgrim** was published by William Jaggard, in 1599. It was a piratical bookseller's venture, and although the popular name of Shakspere was put upon the title-page the little volume really consisted of a collection from several authors. Men-

tion has already been made of the fact that Shakspere, as Heywood tells us, was much offended when Jaggard, in 1612, republished the volume, with added poems of Heywood, and with Shakspere's name upon the title-page: a cancel of the title-page thereupon was made, and one printed without any author's name. After the fifteenth poem of the original collection occurs a second title—*Sonnets to Sundry Notes of Music.* The following table shows, as far as has been ascertained, how the volume was made up (the references are to the *Globe Shakspere*):

I. II. Shakspere's *Sonnets*, 138 and 144 (with various readings, those of the *Sonnets* the true or the later readings).
III. Longaville's sonnet to Maria in *Love's Labour's Lost* (Act IV. Sc. iii. L. 60-73).
IV. (?) Shakspere's (on the subject of *Venus and Adonis*).
V. From *Love's Labour's Lost* (Act IV. Sc. ii. L. 109-122).
VI. (?) Shakspere's (on the subject of *Venus and Adonis*).
VII. (?) Shakspere's.
VIII. Probably by Richard Barnfield, in whose *Poems in Divers Humors*, 1598, it had first appeared.
IX. (?) Shakspere's (on the subject of *Venus and Adonis*).
X. Probably not Shakspere's.
XI. Probably by Bartholomew Griffin, in whose *Fidessa more Chaste than Kinde*, 1596, it had appeared with various readings (on the subject of *Venus and Adonis*).
XII. Perhaps Shakspere's.
XIII. Probably by the same writer as X.
XIV. Probably not Shakspere's.
XV. Probably not Shakspere's.
XVI. Certainly not Shakspere's.
XVII. Dumain's poem to Kate in *Love's Labour's Lost* (Act IV. Sc. iii. L. 101-120).
XVIII. From Weelkes's *Madrigals*, 1597.
XIX. (?) Possibly Shakspere's.
XX. By Marlowe (given here imperfectly), *Love's Answer* (also defective here) is attributed to Sir W. Ralegh.
XXI. By Richard Barnfield, from his *Poems in Divers Humors*, 1598.

22. **The Phœnix and the Turtle** was printed as one of the additional poems to Chester's *Love's*

Martyr, or Rosalin's Complaint, 1601, with Shakspere's name appended. The occasion and subject of this allegorical poem are lost in obscurity.

23. **The Sonnets of Shakspere** suggest, perhaps, the most difficult questions in Shaksperian criticism. In 1609 appeared these poems in a quarto (published almost certainly without the author's sanction), which also contained *A Lover's Complaint*. The publisher, Thomas Thorpe, dedicated them "To the onlie begetter of these ensuing sonnets, Mr. W. H." Does "begetter" mean the person who inspired them and so brought them into existence, or only the obtainer of the *Sonnets* for Thorpe? Probably the former. And who is Mr. W. H.? It is clear from sonnet 135 that the christian-name of Shakspere's friend to whom the first 126 sonnets were addressed was William. But what William? There is not even an approach to certainty in any answer offered to this question. Some have supposed that W. H. is a blind to conceal and yet express the initials H. W., *i.e.* Henry Wriothesley Earl of Southampton, Shakspere's patron; others hold that William Herbert, Earl of Pembroke (to whom, together with his brother, the first folio is dedicated), is here addressed.

When were the *Sonnets* written? We know Meres in 1598 spoke of Shakspere's "sugred sonnets among his private friends," and that in 1599 two (138 and 144) were printed in *The Passionate Pilgrim*. Some, if we were to judge by their style, seem to belong to the time when *Romeo and Juliet* was written. Others—as, for example, 66-74—echo the sadder tone which is heard in *Hamlet* and *Measure for Measure*. The writing of the *Sonnets* certainly extended over a considerable period of time, at least three years (see 104), and perhaps a longer period. They all lie, I believe, somewhere between 1595 and 1605.

The *Sonnets* consist of two series, the first from 1 to 126 (The Envoy, 126, consisting of twelve lines in couplets), addressed to a young man; the other, 127–154, addressed to or referring to a woman. But both series allude to events which connect the two persons with one another and with Shakspere. The young friend, whom Shakspere loved with a fond idolatry, was beautiful, clever, rich in the gifts of fortune, of high rank. The woman was of stained character, false to her husband, the reverse of beautiful, dark-eyed, pale-faced, a musician, possessed of a strange power of attraction. To her fascination Shakspere yielded himself, and in his absence she laid her snares for Shakspere's friend and won him. Hence a coldness, estrangement, and, for some time, a complete severance between Shakspere and his friend, after a time followed by acknowledgment of faults on both sides and a complete reconciliation.

So the *Sonnets* must be interpreted if we accept the natural sense they seem to bear. But several persons have held that they are either altogether of an ideal nature or allegorical, or were written in part by Shakspere not for himself but for the use of others. The natural sense, however, is, I am convinced, the true one.

Sonnets from 1 to 126 form, allowing for a few breaks, a continuous series. In the early Sonnets the poet urges his friend to marry, that, surviving in his children, he may conquer Time the Decay. But if he refuses this, then Verse —the poetry of Shakspere—must make war upon Time, and confer immortality upon his friend's loveliness (15–19).* Many of the poems are written in absence (26, 27, 28, &c.). All Shakspere's griefs and losses are made good to him by joy in his friend (29–31). The wrong done by "Will" to Shakspere is then spoken of (33), for which some "salve" is offered (34); the salve is worthless, but Shakspere will try to forgive. We trace the gradual growth of distrust on

---

* The figures are meant not to mark divisions or groups of sonnets, but to illustrate by striking passages the brief analysis of the *Sonnets*.

each side (58), until a melancholy settles down upon the heart of Shakspere (66). Still he loves his friend, and tries to think him pure and true. Then a new trouble arises: his friend is favouring a rival poet of great learning and skill (76-86). This rival poet has, with some show of evidence, been conjectured to be George Chapman, the translator of Homer. Shakspere bids his friend " Farewell " (87); let him hate Shakspere if he will. He ceases to address poems to him; but after an interval of silence begins once more to sing (100, 101, 102, &c.). He sees his friend again and finds him still beautiful. There is a reconciliation (104, 105, 107). Explanations and confessions are made. Love is restored, stronger than ever (119), for now it has passed through trial and sorrow; it is founded not on interested motives (124), nor, as formerly, on the attraction of youth and beauty, but is inward of the heart (125). And thus, gravely and happily, the *Sonnets* to his friend conclude.

The reader who chooses to investigate the second series of *Sonnets*—those to Shakspere's dark mistress—will meet with little difficulty in understanding them. Perhaps 153, 154, which seem to be two experiments in verse on the same subject, ought to be placed apart from the rest.

Having introduced the *Sonnets* here, as the appearance of two of the series in *The Passionate Pilgrim* suggested, we now return to the comedies; and the *Sonnets* may be considered to have been viewed from a mid-point in the period of their composition, from which their retrospective and prospective significance may become apparent.

24. **Twelfth Night**, we learn from Manningham's *Diary*, was acted at the Middle Temple, February 2, 1601-1602. Steevens supposed that " the new map, with the augmentation of the Indies," spoken of by Maria (Act III. Sc. ii. L. 86), had reference to the map in Linschoten's *Voyages*, 1598. The date of the play is probably 1600-1601.

Manningham writes of the play: "Much like *The Comedy of Errors* or *Menechmi* in Plautus, but most like and neere to that in Italian called *Inganni*." There are two Italian plays of an earlier date than *Twelfth Night*, entitled *Gl' Inganni* (*The Cheats*), containing incidents in some degree resembling those of Shakspere's comedy, and in that by Gonzaga, the sister who assumes male attire, producing thereby confusion of identity with her brother, is named Cesare (Shakspere's Cesario). But a third Italian play, *Gl' Ingannati*, presents a still closer resemblance to *Twelfth Night*, and in its poetical induction, *Il Sacrificio*, occurs the name Malevolti (Malvolio). The story is told in Bandello's novel (ii. 36), and was translated by Belleforest into French, in *Histoires Tragiques*. Whether Shakspere consulted any Italian source or not, he had doubtless before him the version of the story (from Cinthio's *Hecatomithi*) by Barnabe Rich—the *Historie of Apolonius and Silla* in *Riche His Farewell to Militarie Profession* (1581)—and this, in the main, he followed. The characters of Malvolio, Sir Toby Belch, Sir Andrew Aguecheek, Fabian, the clown Feste, and Maria, with the part they play in the comedy, are creations of Shakspere.

No comedy of Shakspere's unites such abounding mirth and fine satire, with the charm of a poetical romance. It is the summing up of the several admirable qualities which appear in the joyous comedies, of which it forms the last. An edge is put on the roystering humour of Sir Toby by the sharp waiting-maid wit of Maria, which saves it from becoming an aimless rollicking. Sir Andrew is a Slender grown adult in brainlessness, and who has forgotten that he is not as richly endowed by nature as by fortune; and yet he is visited by a glimmering suspicion that others may think he is an ass, which obliges him to air his incapacity and give it importance. Feste, the clown, is less quaint than Touchstone, but more versatile, less a contemplative fool, and more actively a lover of jest and waggery. Among this abandoned crew of topers and drolls stalks the solemn "yellow-legged stork" Malvolio. His sense of self-importance has diffused itself over all the details of life, so that the whole of human existence, as he would have it, must become as pompous and as exemplary as the manners of my lady's steward. The cruelty of his deception and disillusion is in proportion to the greatness of his distempered self-esteem.

The Duke Orsino is infected with the lover's melancholy, which is fantastical and nice. He nurses his love and dallies with it, and tries to yield up all his consciousness to it, as to a delicious sensation; and therefore his love is not quite earnest or deep; it is like the colour in an opal; and the loss of Olivia is but the loss of a fair vision, which is replaced by one as fair and more real. Olivia has not the love-languor of the Duke, but her resolved sorrow for her lost brother, so soon forgotten in a stronger feeling, shows a little of the same unreality of self-conscious emotion which we perceive in the Duke's love; she is of a nature harmonious and refined, but is too much a child of wealth and ease to win away our chief interest from the heroine of the play. Viola is like a heightened portrait of the Julia of *The Two Gentlemen of Verona*, enriched with lovely colour and placed among more poetical surroundings. She has not the pretty sauciness of Rosalind in her disguise, but owns a heart as tender, sweet-natured, and sound-natured as even Rosalind's. The mirth of the play belongs to other actors than Viola; her occasional playfulness falls back into her deep tenderness and is lost in it.

It has been suggested (see Hunter: *New Illustrations of Shakespeare*, vol. i. p. 380) that Shakspere ridicules, in the scene between the clown, as Sir Topas, and Malvolio, the exorcisms by Puritan ministers, in the case of a family named Starchy

(1596-99), and that the difficult word Strachy (Act II. Sc. v. L. 45) was a hint to the audience to expect subsequent allusion to the Starchy affair. But all this is highly doubtful.

25. **Julius Cæsar** was produced as early as 1601; so we infer from the passage quoted p. 34, from Weever's *Mirror of Martyrs*. In Drayton's *Barons' War*, 1603, occurs a passage which closely resembles some lines of the speech of Antony over Brutus' body (last scene of the play). The style of the versification, the diction, the characterisation, all bear out the opinion that 1600 or 1601 is the date of *Julius Cæsar*. The historical materials of the play were found by the dramatist in the lives of Cæsar, of Brutus, and of Antony, as given in North's translation of Plutarch. Hints for the speeches of Brutus and Antony seem to have been obtained from Appian's *Civil Wars*, B. II. ch. 137-147, translated into English in 1578.

Everything is wrought out in the play with great care and completeness; it is well planned and well proportioned; there is no tempestuousness of passion, and no artistic mystery. The style is full, but not overburdened with thought or imagery; this is one of the most perfect of Shakspere's plays; greater tragedies are less perfect, perhaps for the very reason that they try to grasp greater, more terrible, or more piteous themes.

In *King Henry V*. Shakspere had represented a great and heroic man of action. In the serious plays, which come next in chronological order, *Julius Cæsar* and *Hamlet*, the poet represents two men who were forced to act—to act in public affairs, and affairs of life and death—yet who were singularly disqualified for playing the part of men of action. Hamlet cannot act because his moral energy is sapped by a kind of scepticism and sterile despair about life, because his own ideas are more to him than deeds, because his will is diseased. Brutus does act, but he acts as an idealist and theoriser might, with no eye for the actual bearing of facts, and no sense of the true importance of persons. Intellectual doctrines and moral ideals rule the life of Brutus; and his life is most noble, high, and stainless, but his public action is a series of practical mistakes. Yet even while he errs we admire him, for all his errors are those of a pure and lofty spirit. He fails to see how full of power Antony is, because Antony loves pleasure, and is not a Stoic, like himself; he addresses calm arguments to the excited Roman mob; he spares the life of Antony and allows him to address the people; he advises ill in military matters. All the practical gifts, insight and tact, which Brutus lacks, are possessed by Cassius; but of Brutus's moral purity, veneration of ideals, disinterestedness, and freedom from unworthy personal motive, Cassius possesses little. And the moral power of Brutus has in it something magisterial, which enables it to oversway the practical judgment of Cassius. In his wife—Cato's daughter, Portia—Brutus has found one who is equal to and worthy of himself. Shakspere has shown her as perfectly a woman—sensitive, finely-tempered, tender—yet a woman who by her devotion to moral ideals might stand beside such a father and such a husband. And Brutus, with all his Stoicism, is gentle and tender: he can strike down Cæsar if Cæsar be a tyrant, but he cannot roughly rouse a sleeping boy (Act IV. Sc. iii. L. 270). Antony is a man of genius, with many splendid and some generous qualities, but self-indulgent, pleasure-loving, and a daring adventurer, rather than a great leader of the State.

The character of Cæsar is conceived in a curious and almost irritating manner. Shakspere (as passages in other plays show) was certainly not ignorant of the greatness of one of the world's greatest men. But here it is his weaknesses that are insisted on. He is failing in body and mind, influenced by superstition, yields to flattery, thinks of himself as almost superhuman, has lost some of his insight into character, and his sureness and swiftness of action. Yet the play is rightly named *Julius Cæsar*. His bodily presence is weak, but his spirit rules throughout the play, and rises after his death in all its might, towering over the little band of conspirators, who at length fall before the spirit of Cæsar as it ranges for revenge.

26. **Hamlet** represents the mid period of the growth of Shakspere's genius, when comedy and history ceased to be adequate for the expression of his deeper thoughts and sadder feelings about life, and when he was entering upon his great series of tragic writings. In July, 1602, the printer Roberts entered in the Stationers' register, "The Revenge of Hamlett, Prince of Denmark, as y^t latelie was acted by the Lord Chamberlain his servantes," and in the next year the play was printed. The true relation of this first quarto of *Hamlet* to the second quarto, published in 1604—"newly imprinted, and enlarged to almost as much againe as it was"—is a matter in dispute. It is believed by some critics that the quarto of 1603 is merely an imperfect report of the play as we find it in the edition of the year after; but there are some material differences which cannot thus be explained. In the earlier quarto, instead of Polonius and Reynaldo, we find the names Corambis and Montano; the order of certain scenes varies from that of the later quarto; "the madness of Hamlet is much more pronounced, and the Queen's innocence of her husband's murder much more explicitly stated." We are forced to believe either that the earlier quarto contains portions of an old play by some other writer than Shakspere— an opinion adopted on apparently insufficient grounds by some recent editors—or that it represents imperfectly Shakspere's first draught of the play, and that the difference between it and the second quarto is due to Shakspere's revision of his own work. This last opinion seems to be the true one, but the value of any comparison between the two quartos,

with a view to understand Shakspere's manner of rehandling his work, is greatly diminished by the fact that numerous gaps of the imperfect report given in the earlier quarto seem to have been filled in by a stupid stage hack. That an old play on the subject of Hamlet existed there can be no doubt; it is referred to in 1589 (perhaps in 1587) by Nash, in his *Epistle* prefixed to Greene's *Menaphon*, and again in 1596, by Lodge (*Wit's Miserie and the World's Madnesse*), where he alludes to "the visard of the Ghost which cried so miserably at the Theator, like an oister wife, 'Hamlet, reuenge.'" A German play on the subject of Hamlet exists, which is supposed to have been acted by English players in Germany in 1603; the name Corambus appears in it; and it is possible that portions of the old pre-Shaksperian drama are contained in the German *Hamlet*. The old play may have been one of the bloody tragedies of revenge among which we find *Titus Andronicus* and *The Spanish Tragedy*, and it would be characteristic of Shakspere that he should refine the motives and spirit of the drama, so as to make the duty of vengeance laid upon Hamlet a painful burden which he is hardly able to support.

One additional point must be noted with reference to the date of the play. In Act II. Sc. ii. L. 346, Rosencrantz explains that the tragedians of the city are compelled to travel on account of an "inhibition" which is caused by "the late innovation." What does this mean? Does it allude to the Order in Council of June, 1600, limiting the number of playhouses about London to two, an order not carried out until the duty of enforcing it was urged upon the justices of Middlesex and Surrey, December 31, 1601? Or shall we understand "the innovation" as referring to the licence given January 1603-1604, to the children of the Queen's Revels to play at the Blackfriars Theatre—a building belonging to the company of which Shakspere was a member? The licence to the children (of whom

Rosencrantz speaks depreciatingly) would act as an inhibition to the company of adult actors whose place they occupied.

Beside the old play of Hamlet, Shakspere had probably before him the prose *Hystorie of Hamblet* (though no edition exists earlier than 1608), translated from Belleforest's *Histoires Tragiques*. The story had been told some hundreds of years previously, in the *Historia Danica* of Saxo Grammaticus (ab. 1180-1208). The Hamlet of the *Hystorie*, after a fierce revenge, becomes King of Denmark, marries two wives, and finally dies in battle.

No play of Shakspere's has had a higher power of interesting spectators and readers, and none has given rise to a greater variety of conflicting interpretations. It has been rightly named a tragedy of thought, and in this respect, as well as others, takes its place beside *Julius Cæsar*. Neither Brutus nor Hamlet is the victim of an overmastering passion as are the chief persons of the later tragedies—*e.g.* Othello, Macbeth, Coriolanus. The burden of a terrible duty is laid upon each of them, and neither is fitted for bearing safely the burden. Brutus is disqualified for action by his idealism, his student-like habits, his capacity for dealing with abstractions rather than with men and things. Hamlet is disqualified for action by his excess of the reflective tendency, and by his unstable will, which alternates between complete inactivity and fits of excited energy. Naturally sensitive, he receives a painful shock from the hasty second marriage of his mother; already the springs of faith and joy in his nature are embittered; then follows the terrible discovery of his father's murder, with the injunction laid upon him to revenge the crime; upon this again follow the repulses which he receives from Ophelia. A deep melancholy lays hold of his spirit, and all of life grows dark and sad to his vision. Although hating his father's murderer, he has little heart to push on his revenge. He is aware that he is suspected and surrounded by spies. Partly to baffle them, partly to create a veil behind which to seclude his true self, partly because his whole moral nature is indeed deeply disordered, he assumes the part of one whose wits have gone astray. Except for one loyal friend, he is alone among enemies or supposed traitors. Ophelia he regards as no more loyal or honest to him than his mother had been to her dead husband. The ascertainment of Claudius's guilt by means of the play still leaves him incapable of the last decisive act of vengeance. Not so, however, with the king, who now recognising his foe in Hamlet, does not delay to despatch him to a bloody death in England. But there is in Hamlet a terrible power of sudden and desperate action. From the melancholy which broods over him after the burial of Ophelia he rouses himself to the play of swords with Laertes, and at the last, with strength which leaps up before its final extinction, he accomplishes the punishment of the malefactor.

Horatio, with his fortitude, his self-possession, his strong equanimity, is a contrast to the Prince. And Laertes, who takes violent measures at the shortest notice to revenge *his* father's murder, is in another way a contrast; but Laertes is the young gallant of the period, and his capacity for action arises in part from the absence of those moral checks of which Hamlet is sensible. Polonius is owner of the shallow wisdom of this world, and exhibits this grotesquely while now on the brink of dotage; he sees, but cannot see through Hamlet's ironical mockery of him. Ophelia is tender, sensitive, affectionate, but the reverse of heroic; she fails Hamlet in his need, and then in her turn becoming the sufferer, gives way under the pressure of her afflictions. We do not honour, we commiserate her.

The play is hardly consistent with respect to Hamlet's age. In Act V. Sc. i. L. 155–191, it is stated that he is thirty years old, while in the first Act he is spoken of as still quite youthful; yet only a few months, at most, can have elapsed in the interval of time between the beginning and the end of the action. His profoundly reflective soliloquies point to an age certainly past early youth.

27. **All's Well that Ends Well.**—Among the plays of Shakspere mentioned by Meres in his *Palladis Tamia* (1598) occurs the name of *Love's Labour's Won*. This has been identified by some critics with *The Taming of the Shrew*, by some with *Much Ado about Nothing*. But the weight of authority inclines to the opinion that under this title Meres spoke of the play known to us as *All's Well that Ends Well*. It seems not improbable that *All's Well*, as we possess it in the first folio—and no earlier edition exists—is a rehandling, very thoroughly carried out, of an earlier version of the comedy. Coleridge believed that two styles were discernible in it; there is certainly a larger proportion of rhyming lines in *All's Well* than in any other play completed after the year 1600; and the following rhyming passages have been pointed out as fragments retained from the earlier version: Act I. Sc. i. L. 231-244; Act I. Sc. iii. L. 134-142; Act II. Sc. i. L. 133-213; Act II. Sc. iii. L. 78-111 and 132-151; Act III. Sc. iv. L. 4-17; Act IV. Sc. iii. L. 252-260; Act V. Sc. iii. L. 61-72 and 325-340. It is, however, far from certain that any portion of the play is of early origin, and assigning conjecturally the date about 1602 as that of the completion of the whole, we may view it as belonging to the later group of the second cycle of Shakspere's comedies, not so early, therefore, as *Twelfth Night* or *As You Like It*, and certainly earlier than *Measure for Measure*.

The story of Helena and Bertram was found by Shakspere in Paynter's *Palace of Pleasure* (1566), Paynter having translated it from the *Decameron* of Boccaccio (Novel 9. Third day). Shakspere added the characters of the Countess, Lafeu, Parolles, and the Clown. What interested the poet's imagination in Boccaccio's story was evidently the position and person of the heroine. In Boccaccio, Giletta, the physician's daughter, is inferior in rank to the young Count, Beltramo, but she is rich. Shakspere's Helena is of humbler birth than his Bertram, and she is also poor. Yet poor, and comparatively low-born, she aspires to be the young Count's wife, she pursues him to Paris, and wins him against his will. To show Helena thus reversing in a measure the ordinary relations of man and woman, and yet to show her neither self-seeking nor unwomanly, was the task which the dramatist attempted. On the one hand he insists much on Bertram's youth, and gives him the faults and vices of youth, making the reader or spectator of the play feel that his hero has great need of such a finely-tempered, right-willed and loyal nature to stand by his side as that of Helena. On the other hand he shows us Helena's enthusiastic attachment to Bertram, her fears and cares on his behalf, her adhesion to him rather than to herself, when her husband seems to set their interests in opposition to one another, until we come to feel that the imperious need which makes Helena overstep social conventions is the need of perfect service to the man she loves. When she chooses him her words are:

> I dare not say I take you, but I give
> Me and my service ever while I live
> Into your guiding power.

Bertram's beauty and courage must bear part of the blame of Helena's loving him better than he deserves. With the youthful desire for independence which makes him break away from her, she can intelligently sympathise. In the last Act she appears—when he has entangled himself in falsehood and shame—to save him, and rescue him from his baser self. We feel that when he has at last really found Helena, he is safe, and all ends well. Parolles, the incarnation of bragging meanness, is the counterfoil of Helena—she, the doer of virtuous deeds; he, the utterer of vain and swelling words; she, all brave womanliness; he, too cowardly for manhood. To be delivered from the false friend to whom he adheres, and to be brought into union with the true wife whom he rejects—this is what Bertram needs. Parolles has been compared to Falstaff, but they ought rather to be contrasted; for Sir John is a man of genius, with real wit and power of fascination, and no ridicule can destroy him, but the exposure of Parolles makes him dwindle into his native pitifulness. The Countess is a charming creation of Shakspere; in no play, unless it be some of his latest romantic dramas, is old age made more beautiful and dignified.

The heroine who is the centre of *All's Well that Ends Well*, it will be seen, is singularly clear in judgment and strong in will. If the play was completed about the same time that *Hamlet* reached its final form, the writer could hardly fail to be sensible of the contrast between the hero of his tragedy, so unfitted for action, so irresolute of purpose, and the heroine of his comedy, who always sees the right thing to do, and who always does it, however dangerous, doubtful, or difficult it may be.

28. **Measure for Measure** is one of the darkest and most painful of the comedies of Shakspere, but its darkness is lit by the central figure of Isabella, with her white passion of purity and of indignation against sin. "The wit seems to foam and sparkle up from a fountain of bitterness . . . . . . the humour is made pungent with sarcasm." This play deals with deep things of our humanity—with righteousness and charity, with self-deceit, and moral weakness and strength, even with life and death themselves. All that is soft, melodious, romantic has disappeared from the style; it shows a fearless vigour, penetrating imagination, and much intellectual force and boldness. The date of the play is uncertain. Two passages (Act I. Sc. i. L. 68-73, and Act II. Sc. iv. L. 24-29) have been conjectured to contain "a courtly apology

for King James I.'s stately and ungracious demeanour on his entry into England;" and possibly the revival in 1604 of a statute, which punished with death any divorced person who married again while his or her former husband or wife was living, may have added point to one chief incident in the play.

Shakspere took the story from Whetstone's play *Promos and Cassandra* (1578), and the prose telling of the tale by the same author in his *Heptameron of Civil Discourses* (1582). Whetstone's original was a story in the *Hecatomithi*, of Giraldi Cinthio. Shakspere alters some of the incidents, making the Duke present in disguise throughout, preserving the honour of the heroine, and introducing the character of Mariana to take her wifely place by Angelo as a substitute for Isabella, as in *All's Well that Ends Well* Helena took the place of the widow's daughter, Diana.

This play, like *The Merchant of Venice*, is remarkable for its great pleading scenes; and to Portia's ardour and intellectual force Isabella adds a noble severity of character, a devotion to an ideal of rectitude and purity, and a religious enthusiasm. In Vienna, "where corruption boils and bubbles," appears this figure of virginal strength and uprightness; at the last she is to preside over the sinful city, and perhaps to save it:

> Spirits are not finely touched
> But to fine issues. (Act I. Sc. i. L. 37-38.)

She is almost "a thing ensky'd and sainted," yet she returns from the cloister to the world, there to fill her place as wife and Duchess. Angelo, at the outset, though he must be conscious of the wrong he has done to his betrothed, is more self-deceived than a deceiver. He does not know his own heart, and is severe against others in his imagined superiority to every possible temptation. A terrible abyss is opened to him in the evil passion of his own nature. The unmasking of the self-deceiver here is not, as in the happy comedies, a piece of the mirth of the play; it is painful and stern. The Duke acts throughout as a kind of overruling providence; he has the wisdom of the serpent, which he uses for good ends, and he looks through life with a steady gaze, which results in a justice and even tenderness (although tenderness united with severity) towards others. Claudio is made chiefly to be saved by his sister, but he has a grace of youth, and a clinging enjoyment of life and love, which interest us in him sufficiently for pity, if not for admiration. The minor persons possess each his characteristic feature, but are less important individually than as representatives of the wide-spread social corruption and degradation which surround the chief characters, and form the soil on which they move and the air they breathe. "We never throughout the play get into the free open joyous atmosphere, so invigorating in other works of Shakspere; the oppressive gloom of the prison, the foul breath of the house of shame, are only exchanged for the chilly damp of conventual walls, or the oppressive retirement of the monastery." In a happier world we might turn away from Isabella, but here she is light, strength, and salvation.

29. **Troilus and Cressida** appeared in two quarto editions in the year 1609; on the title-page of the earlier of the two it is stated to have been acted at the Globe; the later contains a singular preface in which the play is spoken of as "never stal'd with the stage, never clapper-claw'd with the palmes of the vulgar," and as having been published against the will of "the grand possessors." Perhaps the play was printed at first for the use of the theatre, and with the intention of being published after having been represented, and that the printers, against the known wish of the proprietors of Shakspere's manuscript, anticipated the first representation and issued the quarto, with the attractive announcement that it was an absolute

novelty. The editors of the folio, after having decided that *Troilus and Cressida* should follow *Romeo and Juliet* among the tragedies, changed their minds, apparently uncertain how the play should be classed, and placed it between the Histories and Tragedies; this led to the cancelling of a leaf, and the filling up of a blank space left by the alteration, with the Prologue to *Troilus and Cressida*—a prologue which is believed by several critics not to have come from Shakspere's hand.

There is extreme uncertainty with respect to the date of the play. Dekker and Chettle were engaged in 1599 upon a play on this subject, and, from an entry in the Stationers' register, February 7, 1602-1603, it appears that a *Troilus and Cressida* had been acted by Shakspere's company, the Lord Chamberlain's Servants. Was this Shakspere's play? We are thrown back upon internal evidence to decide this question, and the internal evidence is itself of a conflicting kind, and has led to opposite conclusions. The massive worldly wisdom of Ulysses argues, it is supposed, in favour of a late date, and the general tone of the play has been compared with that of *Timon of Athens*. The fact that it does not contain a single weak ending, and only six light endings, is, however, almost decisive evidence against our placing it after either *Timon* or *Macbeth*; and the other metrical characteristics are considered, by the most careful student of this class of evidence in the case of the present play (Hertzberg), to point to a date about 1603. Other authorities place it as late as 1608 or 1609; while a third theory (that of Verplanck and Grant White) attempts to solve the difficulties by supposing that it was first written in 1603, and revised and enlarged shortly before the publication of the quarto. Parts of the play—notably the last battle of Hector—appear not to be by Shakspere. The interpretation of the play itself is as difficult as the ascertainment of the external facts of its history. With what intention, and in what spirit did Shakspere write this strange comedy? All the Greek heroes who fought against Troy are pitilessly exposed to ridicule; Helen and Cressida are light, sensual, and heartless, for whose sake it seems infatuated folly to strike a blow; Troilus is an enthusiastic young fool; and even Hector, though valiant and generous, spends his life in a cause which he knows to be unprofitable, if not evil. All this is seen and said by Thersites, whose mind is made up of the scum of the foulness of human life. But can Shakspere's view of things have been the same as that of Thersites?

The central theme, the young love and faith of Troilus given to one who was false and fickle, and his discovery of his error, lends its colour to the whole play. It is the comedy of disillusion. And as Troilus passed through the illusion of his first love for woman, so by middle life the world itself often appears like one that has not kept her promises, and who is a poor deceiver. We come to see the seamy side of life; and from this mood of disillusion it is a deliverance to pass on even to a dark and tragic view of life, to which beauty and virtue reappear, even though human weakness or human vice may do them bitter wrong. Now such a mood of contemptuous depreciation of life may have come over Shakspere, and spoilt him, at that time, for a writer of comedy. But for Isabella we should find the coming on of this mood in *Measure for Measure*; there is perhaps a touch of it in *Hamlet*. At this time *Troilus and Cressida* may have been written, and soon afterwards Shakspere, rousing himself to a deeper inquest into things, may have passed on to his great series of tragedies.

Let us call this, then, the comedy of disillusion, and certainly, wherever we place it, we must notice a striking resemblance in its spirit and structure to *Timon of Athens*. Timon has a lax benevolence and shallow trust in the goodness of men; he is undeceived, and bitterly turns away from the whole human race, in a rage of disappointment. In the same play, Alcibiades is, in like manner, wronged by the world;

but he takes his injuries firmly, like a man of action
and experience, and sets about the subduing of his
base antagonists. Apemantus, again, is the dog-like
reviler of men, knowing their baseness and base himself. Here, Troilus, the noble green-goose, goes
through his youthful agony of ascertaining the unworthiness of her to whom he had given his faith
and hope; but he is made of a stronger and more
energetic fibre than Timon, and comes out of his
trial a man, no longer a boy; somewhat harder,
perhaps, than before, but strung-up for sustained and
determined action. He is completely delivered from
Cressida and from Pandar, and by Hector's death
supplied with a motive for the utmost exertion of his
heroic powers. Ulysses, the antithesis of Troilus, is
the much-experienced man of the world, possessed
of its highest and broadest wisdom, which yet always
remains worldly wisdom, and never rises into the
spiritual contemplation of a Prospero. He sees all
the unworthiness of human life, but will use it for
high worldly ends; the spirit of irreverence and in-
subordination in the camp he would restrain by the
politic machinery of what he calls "degree" (Act I.
Sc. iii. L. 75-136). Cressida he reads at a glance,
seeing to the bottom of her sensual shallow nature,
and he assists at the disillusioning of the young prince,
whose nobleness is apparent to him from the first.
Thersites also sees through the illusions of the world,
but his very incapacity to have ever been deceived is
a sign of the ignoble nature of the wretch. He feeds
and grows strong upon garbage; physical nastiness
and moral sores are the luxuries of his imagination.
The other characters—the brute warrior, Ajax; the
insolent self-worshipper, Achilles; Hector, heroic but
too careless how and when he expends his heroic
strength—are of minor importance. As the blindness
of youthful love is shown in Troilus, so old age, in
its least venerable form, given up to a gratification of
sensuality by proxy, is exposed to derision in Pandar.
The materials for *Troilus and Cressida* were found by

Shakspere in Chaucer's *Troilus and Creseide*, Caxton's translation from the French, *Recuyles, or Destruction of Troy*, perhaps, also, Lydgate's *Troye Boke*. Thersites he probably found in book ii. of Chapman's *Homer*. Shakspere's conception of Cressida and of Pandar differs widely from Chaucer's: in Shakspere's hands, in accordance with the general design of the drama, Cressida and her uncle grow base and contemptible. Some critics have supposed that the love-story was written at a much earlier date than the part which treats of Ulysses; but we have seen that the contrasted characters of Troilus and Ulysses are both essential parts of the conception of the drama, and were created as counterparts.

30. **Othello** is the only play which appeared in quarto (1622) in the interval between Shakspere's death and the publication of the first folio. We have no means, except by internal evidence, of ascertaining the date at which the play was written. Upon the strength of a supposed allusion to the armorial bearings of the new order of Baronets, instituted in 1611—

> The hearts of old gave hands,
> But our new heraldry is hands, not hearts.
> (Act III. Sc. iv. L. 46-47.)—

the play has been referred to a year not earlier than 1611. But the metrical tests confirm the impression produced by the general character and spirit of the tragedy, that it cannot belong to the same period as *The Tempest, Cymbeline*, and *The Winter's Tale*. It evidently is one of the group of tragedies of passion which includes *Macbeth* and *Lear*. The year 1604 has been accepted by several critics as a not improbable date for *Othello*.

The original of the story is found in Cinthio's *Hecatomithi*, but it has been in a marvellous manner elevated and re-created by Shakspere. The incident of an intended attack on Cyprus by the Turks may have been suggested by the historical fact that such an attack was actually made in the year 1570.

Coleridge has justly said that the agonised doubt which lays hold of the Moor is not the jealousy of a man of naturally jealous temper, and he contrasts Othello with Leontes in *The Winter's Tale*, and Leonatus in *Cymbeline*. A mean watchfulness or prying suspicion is the last thing that Othello could be guilty of. He is of a free and noble nature, naturally trustful, with a kind of grand innocence, retaining some of his barbaric simpleness of soul in midst of the subtle and astute politicians of Venice. He is great in simple heroic action, but unversed in the complex affairs of life, and a stranger to the malignant deceits of the debased Italian character. Nothing is more chivalrous, more romantic, than the love of Othello and Desdemona. The beautiful Italian girl is fascinated by the regal strength and grandeur, and tender protectiveness of the Moor. He is charmed by the sweetness, the sympathy, the gentle disposition, the gracious womanliness of Desdemona. But neither quite rightly knows the other; there is none of that perfect equality and perfect knowledge between them which unites so flawlessly Brutus and Portia.

Desdemona and Othello are parted on their voyage to Cyprus, and at meeting their happiness touches a height which is almost too rare and exquisite. From that moment of rapture and reunion to the moment when Othello slays himself by the body of his murdered wife, there is an unalleviated intensity of tragic pain. Othello cannot hate Desdemona; his misery is that he must love her although he strives to hate, and must slay her, although he would die that she might be pure and live. There is no character in Shakspere's plays so full of serpentine power and serpentine poison as Iago. The Iachimo of *Cymbeline* is a faint sketch in water-colours of the absolute villain Iago. He is envious of Cassio, and suspects that the Moor may have wronged his honour; but his malignancy is out of all proportion to even its alleged motives. Cassio, notwithstanding his moral weaknesses, is a chivalrous nature, possessed by enthusiastic admiration of his great general and the beautiful lady who is his wife. But Iago can see neither human virtue nor greatness. All things to him are common and unclean, and he is content that they should be so. He is not the sly, sneaking, and too manifest villain of some of the actors of his part. He is "honest Iago," and passes for a rough yet shrewd critic of life, who is himself frank and candid. To ensnare the nobly guileless Othello was, therefore, no impossible task. Shakspere does not allow Iago to triumph; his end is wretched as his life had been. And Othello, restored to love through such tragic calamity, dies once more reunited to his wife, and loyal, in spite of all his wrongs, to the city of his adoption. It is he who has sinned, and not she who was dearer to him than himself, and of his own wrongs and griefs he can make a sudden end.

Emilia may be compared with Paulina of *The Winter's Tale.*

31. **King Lear,** among the tragedies of passion, is the one in which passions assume the largest proportions, act upon the widest theatre, and attain their absolute extremes. The story of Lear and his daughters was found by Shakspere in Holinshed, and he may have taken a few hints from an old play, *The True Chronicle History of King Leir*, &c. In both Holinshed's version and that of the *True Chronicle*, the army of Lear and his French allies is victorious; Lear is reinstated in his kingdom; but Holinshed relates how, after Lear's death, her sisters' sons warred against Cordelia, and took her prisoner, when "being a woman of a manly courage and despairing to recover liberty," she slew herself. The story is also told by Higgins in *The Mirror for Magistrates*; by Spenser (*Fairie Queene*, II. x. 27–32), from whom Shakspere adopted the form of the name "Cordelia;" and in a ballad (printed in Percy's *Reliques*) probably later in date than Shakspere's play. With the story of Lear Shakspere connects that of Gloucester and his two sons. An episode in Sir Philip Sidney's *Arcadia* sup-

plied characters and incidents for this portion of the play, Sidney's blind king of Paphlagonia corresponding to the Gloucester of Shakspere. But here, too, the story had in the dramatist's original a happy ending: the Paphlagonian king is restored to his throne, and the brothers are reconciled.

The date of Shakspere's play is probably 1605 or 1606. It was entered on the Stationers' register, Nov. 26, 1607, and the entry states that it had been acted "upon St. Stephan's day at Christmas last," *i.e.* Dec. 26, 1606. The play was printed in quarto in 1608. "An upward limit of date is supplied by the publication of Harsnet's *Declaration of Popish Impostures*, 1603, to which Shakspere was indebted for the names of many of the devils in Edgar's speeches." It has been suggested that Gloucester's mention of "late eclipses in the sun and moon" (Act I. Sc. ii. L. 112) refers to the great eclipse of the sun, October, 1605, preceded within a month by an eclipse of the moon, and that the words which follow shortly after the mention of eclipses, "machinations, hollowness, treachery, and all ruinous disorders, follow us disquietly to our graves," had special point if delivered on the stage while the Gunpowder Plot of Nov. 5, 1605, was fresh in men's minds.

Shakspere cares little to give the opening incidents of his play a look of prosaic, historical probability. The spectator or reader is asked, as it were, to grant the dramatist certain data, and then to observe what the imagination can make of them. Good and evil in this play are clearly severed from one another—(more so than in *Macbeth* or in *Othello*)—and at the last, goodness, if we judge merely by external fortune, would seem to be, if not defeated, at least not triumphant. Shakspere has dared, while paying little regard to mere historical verisimilitude, to represent the most solemn and awful mysteries of life as they actually are, without attempting to offer a ready-made explanation of them. Cordelia dies strangled in prison; yet we know that her devotion of love was not misspent. Lear expires in an agony of grief; but he has been delivered from his pride and passionate wilfulness: he has found that instead of being a master, at whose nod all things must bow, he is weak and helpless, a sport even of the wind and the rain; his ignorance of true love, and pleasure in false professions of love, have given place to an agonised clinging to the love which is real, deep, and tranquil because of its fulness. Lear is the greatest sufferer in Shakspere's plays; though so old, he has strength which makes him a subject for prolonged and vast agony; and patience is unknown to him. The elements seem to have conspired against him with his unnatural daughters; the upheaval of the moral world, and the rage of tempest in the air seem to be parts of the same gigantic convulsion. In the midst of this tempest wanders unhoused the white-haired Lear; while his fool—most pathetic of all the minor characters of Shakspere—jests half-wildly, half-coherently, half-bitterly, half-tenderly, and always with a sad remembrance of the happier past. The poor boy's heart has been sore ever since his "young mistress went to France."

If Cordelia is pure love, tender and faithful, and Kent is unmingled loyalty, the monsters Goneril and Regan are gorgons rather than women, such as Shakspere has nowhere else conceived. The aspect of Goneril can almost turn to stone; in Regan's tongue there is a viperous hiss. Goneril is the more formidable, because the more incapable of any hatred which is not solid and four-square. Regan acts under her sister's influence, but has an eager venomousness of her own. The story of Gloucester enlarges the basis of the tragedy. Lear's affliction is no mere private incident; there is a breaking of the bonds of nature and society all around us. But Gloucester is suffering for a former sin of self-indulgence, Lear is "more sinned against than sinning." Yet Gloucester is granted a death which is half joyful. His affliction serves as a measure of the huger affliction of the king.

Edgar and Edmund are a contrasted pair—both are men of penetration, energy, and skill, one on the side of evil, the other on the side of good. Edgar's virtue is active, enduring, and full of device; he rises at last to be the justiciary who brings his evil brother sternly to punishment. Everywhere throughout the play Shakspere's imaginative daring impresses us. Nothing in poetry is bolder or more wonderful than the scene on the night of the tempest in the hovel where the king, whose intellect has now given way, is in company with Edgar, assuming madness, the Fool, with his forced pathetic mirth, and Kent.

The text of the quarto differs considerably from that of the folio; but the opinion that the later text— that of the folio—exhibits a revision of his own work by Shakspere is not supported by sufficient evidence. "The folio was printed from an independent manuscript, and its text is on the whole much superior to that of the quartos. Each, however, supplies passages which are wanting in the other." Scene iii. of Act IV. is not found in the folio.

32. **Macbeth** was seen acted at the Globe by Dr. Forman—who gives a detailed sketch of the play— on April 20, 1610. But the characteristics of versification forbid us to place it after *Pericles* and *Antony and Cleopatra*, or very near *The Tempest*. Light endings begin to appear in considerable number in *Macbeth* (twenty-one is the precise number), but of weak endings it contains only two. Upon the whole, the internal evidence supports the opinion of Malone, that the play was written about 1606. The words in Macbeth's vision of the kings (Act IV. Sc. i. L. 120),

> Some I see
> That twofold balls and treble sceptres carry,

refer to the union of the two kingdoms under James I. James had revived the practice of touching for the king's evil, described Act IV. Sc. iii. L. 140–159. "Here's a farmer that hang'd himself on the expectation of plenty" (Act II. Sc. iii. L. 5) may have reference to the unusually low price of wheat in the summer and autumn of 1606. "Here's an equivocator that could swear in both scales against either scale; who committed treason enough for God's sake; yet could not equivocate to heaven" (Act II. Sc. iii. L. 9) has been supposed to allude to the doctrine of *equivocation*, avowed by Henry Garnet, Superior of the order of Jesuits in England, on his trial for the Gunpowder Treason, March 28, 1606, and to his perjury on that occasion. In 1611 the ghost of Banquo was jestingly alluded to in Beaumont and Fletcher's *Knight of the Burning Pestle*.

The materials for his play Shakspere found in Holinshed's *Chronicle*, connecting the portion which treats of Duncan and Macbeth with Holinshed's account of the murder of King Duffe by Donwald. The appearance of Banquo's ghost and the sleepwalking of Lady Macbeth appear to be inventions of the dramatist.

Thomas Middleton's play of *The Witch*, discovered in MS. in 1779, contains many points of resemblance to *Macbeth*. The Cambridge editors, Messrs. Clark and Wright, are of opinion that *Macbeth* was interpolated with passages by a second author—not improbably by Middleton—after Shakspere's death, or after he had ceased to be connected with the theatre; the interpolator expanded the parts assigned to the weird sisters and introduced a new character, Hecate. The following passages are pointed out as the supposed interpolations: Act I. Sc. ii., iii. L. 1-37; Act II. Sc. i. L. 61, iii. (Porter's part) Act III. Sc. v.; Act IV. Sc. i. L. 39-47 and 125-132, iii. L. 140-159; Act V. (?) ii., v. L. 47-50, viii. L. 32-33 ("Before my body I throw my warlike shield") and 35-75. This theory of interpolation must be considered as in a high degree doubtful, and in particular the Porter's part shows the hand of Shakspere. As to Middleton's *The Witch*, it was probably of later date than Shakspere's play.

While in *Romeo and Juliet* and in *Hamlet* we feel

that Shakspere now began and now left off, and refined upon or brooded over his thoughts, Macbeth seems as if struck out at a heat, and imagined from first to last with unabated fervour. It is like a sketch by a great master in which everything is executed with rapidity and power, and a subtlety of workmanship which has become instinctive. The theme of the drama is the gradual ruin through yielding to evil within and evil without, of a man, who though from the first tainted by base and ambitious thoughts, yet possessed elements in his nature of possible honour and loyalty. The contrast between Macbeth and Lady Macbeth, united by their affections, their fortunes, and their crime, is made to illustrate and light up the character of each. Macbeth has physical courage, but moral weakness, and is subject to excited imaginative fears. His faint and intermittent loyalty embarrasses him—he would have the gains of crime without its pains. But when once his hands are dyed in blood, he hardly cares to withdraw them, and the same fears which had tended to hold him back from murder, now urge him on to double and treble murders, until slaughter, almost reckless, becomes the habit of his reign. At last the gallant soldier of the opening of the play fights for his life with a wild and brute-like force. His whole existence has become joyless and loveless, and yet he clings to existence. Lady Macbeth is of a finer and more delicate nature. Having fixed her eye upon an end—the attainment for her husband of Duncan's crown—she accepts the inevitable means; she nerves herself for the terrible night's work by artificial stimulants; yet she cannot strike the sleeping king who resembles her father. Having sustained her weaker husband, her own strength gives way; and in sleep, when her will cannot control her thoughts, she is piteously afflicted by the memory of one stain of blood upon her little hand. At last her thread of life snaps suddenly. Macbeth, whose affection for her was real, has sunk too far into the apathy of joyless crime to feel deeply her loss. Banquo, the loyal soldier, praying for restraint of evil thoughts which enter his mind as they had entered that of Macbeth, but which work no evil there, is set over against Macbeth, as virtue is set over against disloyalty. The witches are the supernatural beings of terror, in harmony with Shakspere's tragic period, as the fairies of the *Midsummer Night's Dream* are the supernatural beings of his days of fancy and frolic, and as Ariel is the supernatural genius of his latest period. There is at once a grossness, a horrible reality about the witches, and a mystery and grandeur of evil influence.

33. **Antony and Cleopatra**, though by the person of Antony it connects itself with *Julius Cæsar*, is a striking contrast to that play in subject and in style, and is separated from it in the chronological order by a wide interval. In May of the year 1608, Blount (afterwards one of the publishers of the First Folio) entered in the Stationers' register *A Book called Antony and Cleopatra*. This was, not improbably, Shakspere's tragedy. The source of the play is the life of Antonius in North's *Plutarch*. Shakspere had found in *Plutarch* his Brutus almost ready made to his hand; he deemed it necessary to transform and transfigure the Antony of history, stained as he is by crimes not only of voluptuousness but of cruelty. "Of all Shakspere's historical plays," wrote Coleridge, "*Antony and Cleopatra* is by far the most wonderful," and he calls attention to what he terms its "happy valiancy" of style. Shakspere, indeed, nowhere seems a greater master of a great dramatic theme. The moral ideals, the doctrines, the stoical habits and stoical philosophy of Brutus and Portia, are as remote as possible from the sensuous splendours of the life in Egypt, from Antony's careless magnificence of strength, and the beauty, the arts, and endless variety of Cleopatra. Yet, though the tragedy has all the glow and colour of oriental magnificence, it remains true at heart to the moral laws which govern human life. The worship of pleasure by the Egyptian Queen and her paramour is, after all, a failure, even from the first. There is no

true confidence, no steadfast strength of love possible between Antony and his "serpent of old Nile." Each inspires the other with a mastering spirit of fascination, but Antony knows not the moment when Cleopatra may be faithless to him, and Cleopatra weaves her endless snares to retain her power over Antony. The great Roman soldier gradually loses his energy, his judgment, and even his joy in life; at last, the despair of spent forces settles down upon him, and it is only out of despair that he snatches strength enough to fight fiercely when driven to bay. He is the ruin of Cleopatra's magic. Upon Cleopatra herself the genius of Shakspere has been lavished. She is the most wonderful of his creations of women, formed of the greatest number of elements — apparently conflicting elements, yet united by the mystery of life. "To heap up together all that is most unsubstantial, frivolous, vain, contemptible, and variable, till the worthlessness be lost in the magnitude, and a sense of the sublime spring from the very elements of littleness: to do this belonged only to Shakspere, that worker of miracles." While creating, with so much imaginative ardour, his Cleopatra, Shakspere yet stands away from her, and, in a manner, criticises her. Enobarbus, who sees through every wile and guile of the Queen, is, as it were, a chorus to the play, a looker-on at the game; he stands clear of the golden haze which makes up the atmosphere around Cleopatra; and yet he is not a mere critic or commentator (Shakspere never permitting the presence of a person in his drama who is not a true portion of it). Enobarbus himself is under the influence of the charm of Antony, and slays himself because he has wronged his master. The figures of Antony and the Queen are ennobled and elevated by the strong power of attraction, even of devotion, which they exert over those about them —Antony over Enobarbus, Cleopatra over her attendants, Charmian and Iras.

34. **Coriolanus** was written about 1608, as appears from the metrical characteristics. The light-ending

test puts it next after *Antony and Cleopatra*, and it is probable that such is its actual place in the chronological order. Shakspere in his North's *Plutarch* found another subject for tragedy. Having rendered into art the history of the ruin of a noble nature through voluptuous self-indulgence, he went on to represent the ruin of a noble nature through haughtiness and pride. From Egypt, with its splendours, its glow, its revels, its moral licence, we pass back to austere republican Rome. The majestic figure of Volumnia is Shakspere's ideal of the Roman matron. The gentle Virgilia is the most dutiful and tenderly loyal of wives, and her friend Valeria—(how remote from the free-tongued girls of Cleopatra)—is

> The moon of Rome, chaste as the icicle
> That's curdied by the frost from purest snow
> And hangs on Dian's temple.

But, although free from voluptuousness, the condition of Rome is not strong and sound. There is political division between the patricians and plebeians. Shakspere regards the people as an overgrown child with good and kindly instincts; owning a basis of untutored common-sense, but capable of being led astray by its leaders; possessed of little judgment and no reasoning powers, and without capacity for self-restraint. It is not for the people that Shakspere in this play reserves his scorn, but for their tribunes, the demagogues, who mislead and pervert them—a pair of political foxes. Although nobler types of individual character are to be found among the patricians than the plebeians, the dramatist is not blind to the patrician vices, and indeed the whole tragedy turns upon the existence and the influence of these. Coriolanus is by nature of a kindly and generous disposition, but he inherits the aristocratical tradition, and his kindliness strictly limits itself to the circle which includes those of his own rank and class. For his mother he has a veneration approaching to worship; he is content to be a subordinate under Cominius; for the old Menenius he has an almost filial regard; but the people are "slaves," "curs," "minnows." His haughtiness becomes towering, because his personal pride, which in itself is great, is built up over a solid and high-reared pride of class. When he is banished his bitterness arises not only from his sense of the contemptible nature of the adversaries to whom he is forced to yield, but from the additional sense that he has been deserted by his own class, "the dastard nobles." He would henceforward, if possible, be himself alone, standing

> As if a man were author of himself
> And knew no other kin.

And it is in this spirit of revolt against the bonds of society and of nature that he advances against his native city. But his haughtiness cannot really place him above nature. In the presence of his wife, his boy, and his mother, the strong man gives way, and is restored once more to human love. And so his fate comes upon him. To the last something of his pride remains, and the immediate occasion of his death is an outbreak of that sudden passion, springing from his self-esteem, which had already often and grievously wronged him.

Menenius Agrippa is like an earlier Gonzalo of *The Tempest*, an incarnation of humorous common-sense; he has for Coriolanus a fatherly care, regards him with a fatherly admiration, and would if possible save him from himself.

35. **Timon of Athens** is, beyond reasonable doubt, only in part the work of Shakspere. Whether Shakspere worked upon materials furnished by an older play, or whether he left his play a fragment to be completed by another hand, is uncertain: the former supposition is perhaps the correct one, and the older writer may possibly have been George Wilkins. There is a substantial agreement among the best critics as to what portions of the play are Shakspere's and what are not. The following may be

be distinguished, with some confidence, as the non-Shaksperian parts: Act I. Sc. i. L. 189-240, 258-273 (or? from entrance of Apemantus to end of scene), ii. (certainly); Act II. Sc. ii. L. 45-124; all Act III., except Sc. vi. L. 98-115; Act IV. Sc. ii. L. 30-50, (?) iii. L. 292-362, 399-413, 454-543; Act V. (?) Sc. i. L. i.-59, ii., iii.

There is no external evidence which helps to determine the date at which Shakspere wrote his part of the play; but it was probably later than *Macbeth* and earlier than *Pericles*. The year 1607 is a date which cannot be far astray.

The sources from which Shakspere derived an acquaintance with the story of *Timon* were Paynter's *Palace of Pleasure*, a passage in Plutarch's Life of Mark Antony, and, in particular, a dialogue of Lucian. But if Shakspere worked upon an older play, it may have been through it that he obtained the materials which appear to come from Lucian. Another play on the subject of *Timon* existed in 1600, which has been edited by Dyce. It was, in the opinion of Dyce, intended for an academic audience, and there is no evidence sufficient to prove that it had been seen by Shakspere.

Although only a fragment, Shakspere's part of the play is written with the highest dramatic energy. Nothing is more intense than the conception and rendering of Timon's feelings when he turns in hatred from the evil world. The rich Lord Timon has lived in a rose-coloured mist of pleasant delusions. The conferring of favours has been with him a mode of kindly self-indulgence, and he has assumed that everyone is as liberal-hearted and of as easy generosity as he is himself. Out of his pleasant dream he wakes to find the baseness, the selfishness, and ingratitude of the world. And he passes violently over from his former lax philanthropy to a fierce hatred of mankind. The practical Alcibiades sets at once about righting the wrongs which he has suffered. But Timon can only rage and then die. His rage implies the elements of a possible nobleness in him; he cannot acclimatise himself, as Alcibiades can, to the harsh and polluted air of the world; yet the rage also proceeds from a weakness of nature. The dog-like Apemantus accepts, well-contented, the evil which Alcibiades would punish, and from which Timon flies. He barks and snarls, but does not really suffer. The play is a painful one, unrelieved by the presence of beauty or human worth, except such worth as Timon's steward possesses, and this his master blinded by his fierce misanthropy, has no eyes to see.

36. **Pericles** is the first of the group of plays which I have named Romances. Shakspere's portion of the play has something of the slightness of a preliminary sketch. The first two acts are evidently by another writer than Shakspere, and probably the scenes in Act IV. (Sc. ii., v., and vi.), so revolting to our moral feeling, are also to be assigned away from him. What remains (Acts III., IV., V., omitting the scenes just mentioned), is the pure and charming romance of Marina the sea-born child of Pericles, her loss, and the recovery of both child and mother by the afflicted Prince. Whether Shakspere worked upon the foundation of an earlier play, or whether the non-Shaksperian parts of *Pericles* were additions made to what he had written, we cannot say with certainty. It is supposed by some critics that three hands can be distinguished: that of a general reviser who wrote the first two acts and Gower's choruses—possibly the dramatist George Wilkins; that of a second writer who contributed the offensive scenes of Act IV.; and, thirdly, the hand of Shakspere. *Pericles* was entered in the Stationers' register, 1608, by the bookseller Blount, and was published with a very ill-arranged text the next year (1609) by another bookseller, who had, it is believed, surreptitiously obtained his copy. It was not included among the plays given in the first or second folios, but appeared, with six added plays, in the third folio, 1664. The story upon which *Pericles* is founded is that given in Laurence Twine's *Patterne of Painfull Adventures* (1607)—itself a reprint of an early printed

version from the French; given also in Gower's *Confessio Amantis*, and originally written about the fifth or sixth century of our era, in Greek. In all these earlier forms of the tale the name of the prince or king of Tyre is Apollonius, not Pericles. Both Twine and Gower appear to have been made use of by the writers of *Pericles*, and the debt to Gower is acknowledged by his introduction as the "presenter" of the play. It should be noted that in 1608, probably immediately after the production of the play, appeared a novel by George Wilkins, *The Painfull Adventures of Pericles, Prince of Tyre*, which once more tells the story in prose, the version in this instance being in great measure founded upon the play, of which Wilkins himself is conjectured to have been one of the authors.

The drama as a whole is singularly undramatic. It entirely lacks unity of action, and the prominent figures of the opening scenes quickly drop out of the play. A main part of the story is briefly told in rhymed verse by the presenter, Gower, or is set forth in dumb show. But Shakspere's portion is one and indivisible. It opens on shipboard with a tempest, and in Shakspere's later play of storm and wreck he has not attempted to rival the earlier treatment of the subject. "No poetry of shipwreck and the sea," a living poet writes, "has ever equalled the great scene of *Pericles*; no such note of music was ever struck out of the clash and contention of tempestuous elements." Milton, when writing *Lycidas*, the elegy upon his drowned friend, remembered this scene, and one line in particular—

> And humming water shall o'erwhelm thy corpse.

To this rage of storm succeeds the hush of Cerimon's studious chamber, in which the wife of Pericles, tossed ashore by the waves, wakens wonderingly from her trance to the sound of melancholy music. Cerimon, who is master of the secrets of nature, who is liberal in his "learned charity," who held it ever

> Virtue and cunning were endowments greater
> Than nobleness and riches,

is like a first study for Prospero. In the fifth act Marina, so named from her birth at sea, has grown to the age of fourteen years, and is, as it were, a sister of Miranda and Perdita (note in each case the significant name). She, like Perdita, is a child lost by her parents, and, like Perdita, we see her flower-like with her flowers—only these flowers of Marina are not for a merrymaking, but a grave. The melancholy of Pericles is a clear-obscure of sadness, not a gloom of cloudy remorse like that of Leontes. His meeting with his lost Marina is like an anticipation of the scene in which Cymbeline recovers his sons and daughter; but the scene in *Pericles* is filled with a rarer, keener passion of joy. And again, the marvellous meeting between Leontes and Hermione is anticipated by the union of Pericles and his Thaisa. Thus *Pericles* containing the motives of much that was worked out more fully in later dramas, may be said to bear to the Romances somewhat of the same relation which *The Two Gentlemen of Verona* bears to the comedies of love which succeeded it in Shakspere's second dramatic period.

37. **Cymbeline** interweaves with a fragment of British history taken from Holinshed, a story from Boccaccio's *Decameron* (9th Novel of 2nd Day), the Genevra of the Italian novel corresponding to Shakspere's Imogen. The story is told in a tract called *Westward for Smelts*, 1620 (stated by Steevens and Malone to have been published as early as 1603); but Shakspere appears in some way, directly or indirectly, to have made acquaintance with it as given by Boccaccio. It is a singular circumstance that in the 1600 quarto edition of *Much Ado about Nothing*, the opening stage direction runs: "Enter Leonato [and] Innogen his wife;" but no speech is assigned in the comedy to Innogen, nor does her name reappear. Here Imogen is wife to Leonatus Posthumus. The names of the two princes Shakspere found, as well as the king's name, in Holinshed; but the incidents of their having been stolen, and their life

among the mountains of Wales, appear to have been invented by the dramatist.

Dr. Forman records in his MS. *Booke of Plaies and Notes thereof*, that he saw Cymbeline acted; but he gives no date. His book, however, belongs to the years 1610–1611, and the metrical and other internal evidence point to that time as about the period when the drama must have been written. It is loosely constructed, and some passages possess little dramatic intensity. Several critics have questioned whether the vision of Posthumus (Act V. Sc. iv.) is of Shakspere's authorship, and it is certainly poorly conceived and written. Nevertheless, the play is one of singular charm, and contains in Imogen one of the loveliest of Shakspere's creations of female character.

"Posthumus and Imogen" would be a fitter name for the play than *Cymbeline*. The weak king, governed by his strong-minded, ambitious wife, has but a small share in the action; it is designed that the heroine shall have no true father, no friend or protector for a time, except her faithful servant, Pisanio. His children—royal in nature—inherit none of the king's weakness. The Queen transmits to *her* son only her evil disposition, with none of her force of intellect. Cloten is the aristocrat fool, thick-witted, violent, with the coarse conceit of a high-born boor. Imogen has the incredible bad taste to prefer to him "a poor and worthy gentleman," endowed with beautiful gifts of nature, and possessed of all the culture of his time. But Posthumus, with his plain British understanding, parted from his wife, is no match for the craft and cunning of Italy. His faith in Imogen is of a half-romantic kind, unconfirmed by calm and deep acquaintance with her heart: that faith is not subtly poisoned, like the love of Othello, but suddenly, in one brief and desperate encounter, overthrown. His jealousy is not heroic, like Othello's; it shows something of grossness, unworthy of his truer self. In due time penitential sorrow does its work, his nobler nature reasserts itself, and in the final reunion of parent and lost children, the erring husband is also restored to the quick-beating, joyous heart of his wife.

Except grandeur and majesty, which were reserved for Hermione and Queen Katherine, everything that can make a woman lovely is given by the poet to Imogen: quick and exquisite feelings, brightness of intellect, delicate imagination, energy to hate evil, and to right what is wrong, scorn for what is mean or rude, culture, dainty womanly accomplishments, the gift of song, a capacity for exquisite happiness, and no less sensitiveness to the sharpness of sorrow, a power of quick recovery from disaster when the warmth of love breathes upon her once more, beauty of a type which is noble and refined. And her lost brothers are gallant youths, bred happily far from the court, in wilds where their generous instincts and love of freedom and activity find innocent if insufficient modes of gratification. As in all the works of this period, an open-air feeling pervades a great part of the drama; nature, itself joyous and free, ministers to what is beautiful, simple, or heroic in man, while yet by Shakspere nature alone is never anywhere conceived as sufficient to satisfy the heart or the imagination of a human being. With reconciliation and reunion this, like the other Romances, closes. Even Iachimo— a kind of less absolutely evil Iago, suitable to comedy instead of tragedy—must repent and be forgiven.

38. **The Tempest** was probably written late in the year 1610. A few months previously had appeared an account of the wreck of Sir George Somers' ship in a tempest off the Bermudas, entitled *A Discovery of the Bermudas, otherwise called the Ile of Divels, &c.*, written by Silvester Jourdan. Shakspere (Act I. Sc. ii. L. 229) makes mention of "the still-vexed Bermoothes." Several points of resemblance render it probable that Shakspere in writing the play had Jourdan's tract before him. (See preface to Clarendon Press edition of *The Tempest*, pp. 6, 7.) Add to this, that in following Greene's *Pandosto*, as Shakspere does in his *Winter's Tale* (acted 1611), the dramatist turns

aside from it in one important particular—Perdita is *not* cast adrift at sea in a rudderless boat. Why? Probably because Shakspere had already made use of this incident in *The Tempest*. In the Induction to Jonson's *Bartholomew Fair*, 1614, there is what seems an allusion to Shakspere's Caliban of *The Tempest*: "If there be never a *Servant-monster* i' the *Fayre* who can helpe it, he sayes ; nor a nest of *Antiques*? He is loth to make Nature afraid in his *Playes*, like those that beget *Tales, Tempests*, and such like *Drolleries*." The upward limit of date is fixed by a passage (Act II. Sc. i. L. 147–157) in which Gonzalo describes his imaginary commonwealth, borrowed from Florio's translation of Montaigne's *Essays*, published 1603. The striking resemblance of Shakspere's lines beginning "The cloud-capt towers" (Act IV. Sc. i. L. 152) to a passage in the Earl of Stirling's *Tragedie of Darius* (Edinburgh 1603, London 1604) should also be noted.

Beyond the suggestions obtained from Jourdan's tract no source of the story of the play can be pointed out. Mention was made by the poet Collins of a tale called *Aurelio and Isabella* containing the same incidents, but Collins was in this point mistaken ; he may, however, have seen some other Italian story which resembled *The Tempest*. The name Setebos (Sycorax's god, Act I. Sc. ii. L. 373), and perhaps other names of persons, Shakspere found in Eden's *History of Travaile*, 1577. In the absence of evidence as to a source of the play, the most interesting and important fact in connection with the subject is that the German dramatist Jacob Ayrer, who died in 1605, was author of a play, *Die schöne Sidea*, the plot of which has so much in common with the plot of *The Tempest* that it has been supposed that they must have had the same original (see Clarendon Press edition of *The Tempest*, preface, p. 13). In both appear a magician, his only daughter, and an attendant spirit ; in both, the son of his enemy becomes the magician's prisoner, his sword being rendered powerless by magic, and he is made the bearer of logs for his mistress; in both the story ends with reconciliation and the happiness of the lovers. English actors were in Ayrer's town, Nürnberg, in 1604 and 1606; in 1613, English actors performed in German a *Sedea*. Possibly Shakspere, through some company acting in Germany, may have received an account of Ayrer's play.

The Tempest, although far from lacking dramatic or human interest, has something in its spirit of the nature of a clear and solemn vision. It expresses Shakspere's highest and serenest view of life. Prospero, the great enchanter, is altogether the opposite of the vulgar magician. With command over the elemental powers, which study has brought to him, he possesses moral grandeur, and a command over himself, in spite of occasional fits of involuntary abstraction and of intellectual impatience; he looks down on life, and sees through it, yet will not refuse to take his part in it. In Shakspere's early play of supernatural agencies—*A Midsummer Night's Dream*—the "human mortals" were made the sport of the frolic-loving elves; here the supernatural powers attend on and obey their ruler, man. It has been suggested that Prospero, the great enchanter, is Shakspere himself, and that when he breaks his staff, drowns his book, and dismisses his airy spirits, going back to the duties of his dukedom, Shakspere was thinking of his own resigning of his powers of imaginative enchantment, his parting from the theatre, where his attendant spirits had played their parts, and his return to Stratford.

The persons in this play, while remaining real and living, are conceived in a more abstract way, more as types than those in any other work of Shakspere. Prospero is the highest wisdom and moral attainment; Gonzalo is humorous common-sense incarnated; all that is meanest and most despicable appears in the wretched conspirators; Miranda, whose name seems to suggest wonder, is almost an elemental being, framed in the purest and simplest type of womanhood, yet made substantial by contrast with Ariel, who is an unbodied joy, too much a creature of light and air to know human affection or human sorrow; Caliban —the name formed from cannibal (?)—stands at the other extreme, with all the elements in him—appetites, intellect, even imagination—out of which man emerges into early civilisation, but with a moral nature that is still gross and malignant. Over all presides Prospero like a providence. And the spirit of reconciliation, of forgiveness, harmonising the contentions of men, appears in *The Tempest* in the same noble manner that it appears in *The Winter's Tale, Cymbeline*, and *Henry VIII*. (See Mr. Brooke's Primer: *English Literature*, p. 86, 87.)

Shakspere seems in this play, among other things, to consider the question: What is true freedom? Ariel, unable of human bonds, pants for liberty; Caliban sings his drunken song of freedom, and conspires to throw off the yoke of Prospero's rule; but Ferdinand, the lover, finds true freedom in service to her he loves; and Prospero, resigning his magic powers, finds it in the law of human duty.

The conception of Caliban, it may be noted, had occurred to Shakspere when he wrote *Troilus and Cressida* (Act III. Sc. iii. L. 264). The action of *The Tempest* is comprised within three hours.

The Winter's Tale was seen at the Globe on May 15, 1611, by Dr. Forman, and is described in his MS. *Booke of Plaies and Notes thereof*. The versification is that of Shakspere's latest group of plays; no five-measure lines are rhymed; run-on lines and double endings are numerous. The tone and feeling of *The Winter's Tale* place it in the same period with *The Tempest* and *Cymbeline*; its breezy air is surely that which blew over Warwickshire fields upon Shakspere now returned to Stratford; its country lads and lasses, and their junketings, are those with which the poet had in a happy spirit renewed his acquaintance. It is perhaps the last complete play that Shakspere wrote.

Like the romantic pastoral of Shakspere's mid-period of authorship, *As You Like It*, this comedy is founded upon the tale of an early contemporary of the poet—upon Greene's *Pandosto*, or, as it was afterwards named, *Dorastus and Fawnia*, first published in 1588. The idea of introducing Time as a chorus comes from Greene, and all the principal characters, except Paulina and the incomparable rogue Autolycus. As if to prove his right to deal as he pleased with the dramatic unity of time, Shakspere includes all the incidents of *The Tempest* within the period of three hours, while the spectator of *The Winter's Tale* sees Perdita first as a babe, and afterwards as a maiden of sixteen about to become a wife. In Greene's tale, Bellaria, whom Shakspere has named Hermione, dies upon hearing of the loss of her son; in Shakspere's play she lives to be reunited to her repentant husband.

After his manner, Shakspere drives forward to what chiefly interests him in the subject. The jealousy of Leontes is not a detailed dramatic study like the love and jealousy of Othello. It is a gross madness which mounts to the brain, and turns Leontes' whole nature into unreasoning passion. The character of the noble sufferer Hermione is that with which the dramatist is above all concerned—this first; and, secondly, the grace, beauty, and girlish happiness of Perdita; while of the subordinate persons of the drama, Shakspere delights chiefly in his own creation, Autolycus, the most charming of rogues and rovers. Hermione may be placed side by side with the Queen Katharine of *Henry VIII.*, which play belongs to this period. Both are noble sufferers, who by the dignity and purity of their natures transcend all feeling of vulgar resentment. Deep and even quick feeling never renders Hermione incapable of an admirable justice, nor deprives her of a true sense of pity for him who so gravely wrongs both her and himself. The meeting of kindred, with forgiveness and reconciliation, if these are called for by past offences, forms the common ending of the last plays of Shakspere. The return to life of the lost Hermione is, as it were, set visibly before our eyes; we assist at the reanimating of one who had become a monumental memory; for her recovered daughter she has words of tenderness; her husband she embraces in silence, and we know that the forgiveness is without reserve.

Perdita belongs to the group of exquisite youthful figures set over against those of their graver and sadder elders in the plays of this period. She is one of the same company with Miranda and Marina, and the youthful sons of Cymbeline. The shepherdess-princess, "queen of curds and cream," is less a vision than Miranda, the child of wonder, but more perhaps a creature of this earth. There is nothing lovelier or more innocently joyous in poetry than Perdita at the rustic merry-making, sharing her flowers with old and young. And in Florizel she has found a lover, full of the innocence and chivalry of unstained early manhood.

Autolycus stands by himself among the creations of the dramatist. The art of thieving as practised by him is no crime, but the gift of some knavish god. He does not trample on the laws of morality, but dances or leaps over them with so nimble a foot that we forbear to stay him. In the sad world which contains a Leontes and can lose a Mamillius, so light-hearted a wanderer must be pardoned even if he be light-fingered, and sometimes mistakes for his own the sheet bleaching on the hedge, which happens to be ours. The name Autolycus Shakspere probably found in Golding's translation of Ovid's *Metamorphoses*.

40. **King Henry VIII.**, as we learn from Sir Henry Wotton and from T. Lorking, was being enacted as a new play at the Globe Theatre, under the name *All is True*, in June, 1613, when some burning paper shot off from a cannon set fire to the thatch and occasioned the destruction of the building. It has been shown conclusively by Mr. Spedding (*Gentlemen's Magazine*, Aug., 1850, reprinted in *New Shakspere*

Society's Transactions, 1874) that the play is in part from Shakspere's hand, in part from Fletcher's. A German critic (Hertzberg) has described *Henry VIII.* as "a chronicle-history with three and a half catastrophes, varied by a marriage and a coronation pageant, ending abruptly with the baptism of a child." It is indeed incoherent in structure. After all our sympathies have been engaged upon the side of the wronged Queen Katharine, we are called upon to rejoice in the marriage triumph of her rival, Anne Bullen. "The greater part of the fifth act, in which the interest ought to be gathering to a head, is occupied with matters in which we have not been prepared to take any interest by what went before, and on which no interest is reflected by what comes after." But viewed from another side, that of its metrical workmanship, the play is equally deficient in unity, and indeed betrays unmistakably the presence of two writers. Fletcher's verse had certain strongly-marked characteristics, one of which is the very frequent occurrence of double endings. A portion of *Henry VIII.* is written in the verse of Fletcher, and a portion as certainly in Shakspere's verse. Going over the play, scene by scene, Mr. Spedding arrived at the following result:

Shakspere's part: Act I. Sc. i., ii.; Act II. Sc. iii., iv.; Act III. Sc. ii. (to exit of the king), Act V. Sc. i. The rest of the play is by Fletcher.

In Shakspere's part the proportion of double endings is 1 to 3; in Fletcher's, 1 to 1·7 (SPEDDING); in Shakspere's part the proportion of unstopt lines is 1 to 2·03; in Fletcher's, 1 to 3·79 (FURNIVAL); in Shakspere's part there are 45 light endings and 37 weak endings; in Fletcher's, 7 light endings and 1 weak ending (INGRAM); in Shakspere's part there are six rhymes, *all accidental*; in Fletcher's, ten rhymes (FLEAY).

Upon what plan were the joint labours of Shakspere and Fletcher conducted? The following is Mr. Spedding's conjecture: "It was not unusual in those days, when a play was wanted in a hurry, to set two or three, or even four hands, at work upon it; and the occasion of the Princess Elizabeth's marriage (February, 1612–1613) may very likely have suggested the production of a play representing the marriage of Henry VIII. and Anne Bullen. . . . . I should conjecture that Shakspere had conceived the idea of a great historical drama on the subject of Henry VIII., which would have included the divorce of Katharine, the fall of Wolsey, the rise of Cranmer, the coronation of Anne Bullen, and the final separation of the English from the Romish Church, which being the one great historical event of the reign, would naturally be chosen as the focus of poetic interest; that he had proceeded in the execution of this idea as far, perhaps, as the third act. . . . . when finding that his fellows of the Globe were in distress for a new play to honour the marriage of the Lady Elizabeth with, he thought that his half-finished work might help them, and accordingly handed them his manuscript to make what they could of it; that they put it into the hands of Fletcher (already in high repute as a popular and expeditious playwright), who, finding the original design not very suitable to the occasion, and utterly beyond his capacity, expanded the three acts into five, by interspersing scenes of show and magnificence, and passages of description and long poetical conversations, in which his strength lay . . . . and so turned out a splendid 'historical masque or show-play,' which was, no doubt, very popular then, as it has been ever since."

There are three great figures in the play clearly and strongly conceived by Shakspere: The King, Queen Katharine, and Cardinal Wolsey. The Queen is one of the noble, long-enduring sufferers, just-minded, disinterested, truly charitable, who give their moral gravity and grandeur to Shakspere's last plays. She has clear-sighted penetration to see through the Cardinal's cunning practice, and a lofty indignation against what is base, but no unworthy personal resentment. Henry, if we judge him sternly, is cruel and self-indulgent; but Shakspere will hardly allow us to judge Henry sternly. He is a lordly figure, with a full, abounding strength of nature, a self-confidence, an ease and mastery of life, a power of effortless sway, and seems born to pass on in triumph over those who have fallen and are afflicted. Wolsey is drawn with superb power: ambition, fraud, vindictiveness, have made him their own, yet cannot quite ruin a nature possessed of noble qualities. It is hard at first to refuse to Shakspere the authorship of Wolsey's famous soliloquy in which he bids his greatness farewell (Act III. Sc. ii. L. 350–372), but it is certainly Fletcher's, and when one has perceived this, one perceives also that it was an error ever to suppose it written in Shakspere's manner. The scene in which the vision appears to the dying Queen is also Fletcher's, and in his highest style. We can see from the play that if Shakspere had returned at the age of fifty to the historical drama, the works written then would have been greater in moral grandeur than those written from his thirtieth to his thirty-fifth years.

Henry VIII., as the verse tests show, was probably written after *Winter's Tale*, 1611, and it must of course have been written before June 1613. The name *All is True*, under which it was acted in that year, is referred to in the prologue to the play.

Of doubtful plays two may be noticed:

41. **Doubtful Plays.**—(i.) *The Two Noble Kinsmen* was printed in quarto, 1634, on the title-page of which edition the play is stated to have been written by "the admirable worthies of their time, Mr. John Fletcher and Mr. William Shakspeare." One feels upon reading it that there are certainly two authors. Fletcher's hand is present beyond any doubt; and if the second writer were not Shakspere, we have to ask wonderingly: Who could he have been? Who could have written in a manner which is so like the manner of *Cymbeline*, except the author of *Cymbeline*? A division of the play between the two writers was made by Mr. Hickson, chiefly upon grounds furnished by the differences

of style. The following portions were assigned by him to Shakspere: Act I., except parts of Sc. ii., which was either written by Shakspere and Fletcher in conjunction, or by Fletcher, and revised by Shakspere; Act II. Sc. i.; Act III. Sc. i., ii.; Act IV. Sc. iii.; Act V. (except Sc. ii). This division was subsequently confirmed by Mr. Fleay's application of the double-ending test, by Mr. Furnivall's application of the stopped-line test, and by Professor Ingram's application of the weak-ending test. It must be noted, however, that while the evidence of the presence of two hands in the play is convincing, the most competent critics hesitate to make the assertion that either of the writers was Shakspere. The following figures exhibit the results of the verse test: Light endings, Shakspere's part, 1 in 21; Fletcher's, 1 in 445; weak endings, Shakspere's part, 1 in 32, Fletcher's, 1 in 1426. Unstopped lines, Shakspere's part, 1 in 2·1; Fletcher's, 1 in 5·26. Double endings, Shakspere's part, 1 in 3·4; Fletcher's, 1 in 1·9. In the main the division made by Professor Spalding in his *Letter on Shakspere's Authorship of Two Noble Kinsmen* (reprinted by the New Shakspere Society, 1876), and by Mr. Littledale in his admirable edition of the play (New Shakspere Society, 1876) agrees with that of Mr. Hickson.

The Shakspere portions of the play will repay a careful study. The characterisation may be faint, but there are animated pieces of dialogue, magnificent single speeches, and remarkable Shaksperian turns of expression and imagery. The story is derived from Chaucer's *Knightes Tale*. The underplot of Fletcher, made up of indecency and of trash in about equal proportions, is but slightly connected with the nobler portion of the drama. Shakspere's portion was probably written before his latest fragment—that of *Henry VIII*. He was at this time abandoning dramatic authorship, and seems to have been willing that Fletcher should be the heir to his genius.

(ii.) *Edward III*.—It has been held by some critics

that, in this play, the episode of King Edward's attempt upon the honour of the Countess of Salisbury—nobly repulsed by her—is by Shakspere, *i.e.* from the entrance of the King, Act I. Sc. ii. to end of Act II. The play was entered in the Stationers' register, Dec. 1, 1595, and was published in the following year. If, therefore, any portion was from Shakspere's hand, it is of early date. The question of Shakspere's authorship of the episode must be said to remain up to the present in doubt. *Edward III.* is reprinted in the Tauchnitz edition of *Doubtful Plays of Shakespeare.*

(iii.) Other plays which have been ascribed to Shakspere are *Fair Emm, George-a-Green, The Merry Devil of Edmonton, Arden of Feversham, Mucedorus, The Birth of Merlin, 'Larum for London, Warning for Fair Women.* Add the list from the Third Folio (p. 30). If any one of these has any claim to be considered, even in part, Shakspere's, it is the *Yorkshire Tragedy.*

CHAPTER VII.

SHAKSPERE FROM 1616 TO 1877.

1. **1616 to 1642.**—During Shakspere's life he was upon the whole the most steadily popular playwright of his time; but for awhile the slighter sentiment and the novel plots of Beaumont and Fletcher may have proved more attractive with the public. Ben Jonson, who survived Shakspere for many years, gathered about him a school of younger writers, and though never a great favourite with the people, was looked up to as a master by those who cared more for vigorous thought and a scholarly style than for human passion and imaginative truth. The publication, however, of two folio editions of Shakspere's plays within nine years of each other, proves the interest still taken in

his writings; and prefixed to the second folio is an enthusiastic tribute from a young poet, whose homage was alone worth that of a multitude—the first published verses of John Milton. We know also that one whom Milton did not honour—Charles I.—agreed with Milton in honouring Shakspere, and that his plays were frequently represented at St. James's and Whitehall.

2. **The Restoration Period.**—The civil wars and the victory of Puritanism were, of course, unfavourable to the culture of dramatic poetry. In 1642 the theatres were closed, and they remained so (excepting some irregular performances) until the latter end of the year 1659. During Charles II.'s reign there were two currents of feeling with reference to Shakspere and the Elizabethan drama; it was impossible to deny the power and attraction of the works of the greatest English dramatic poet, but French tastes had begun to prevail, and much in Shakspere appeared antiquated, rude, inartistic, almost barbarous. Davenant, who was not unwilling to be supposed a natural son of Shakspere, revived the great tragedies and some of the comedies and histories; Killigrew's new theatre opened with *Henry IV.*; the wonderful actor Betterton appeared as Hamlet in the first play of Shakspere represented after the Restoration, and (actresses now taking the female parts) Mrs. Betterton played with her husband. For her Ophelia hints were received from Davenant, drawn from his memory of the boy-Ophelias of an earlier time; but her most celebrated Shaksperian character was Lady Macbeth. There is abundant evidence of Shakspere's popularity after the Restoration; it now, however, began to be thought needful to reform Shakspere to suit the taste of a refined and ingenious public. The attractions of spectacle and music were added to those of dramatic poetry. Dryden and Davenant altered *The Tempest* into *The Enchanted Island*, with song and show, with new characters ridiculously out of keeping with the original play, and the added zest of indecency. The method of improving Shakspere to please the town

continued to be applied to his plays with remorseless zeal during a long period of time. Songs were added to *Macbeth*; *Much Ado about Nothing* and *Measure for Measure* were mingled, and out of the mingled material was produced Davenant's *Law against Lovers*. Dennis metamorphosed *The Merry Wives* into *The Comical Gallant*; Durfey altered *Cymbeline*; *Richard II.* became *The Sicilian Usurper*; Tate improved upon *King Lear* by introducing love-passages between Edgar and Cordelia, and giving the play a happy ending; Lord Lansdowne made a comic personage of Shylock; Colley Cibber rehandled *Richard III.*, and introduced some of the rants and time-honoured hits which have been repeated on the stage until our own day. Dryden (to return to Restoration times) both praises and depreciates Shakspere, but as he grew older his admiration for Shakspere increased; the dramatic work of his own, which Dryden most highly valued, *All for Love*, is written in professed imitation of "the divine Shakspere;" and his prose prefaces, which are often critical essays, contain some admirable remarks upon the genius of his great predecessor. Some of Mr. Pepys's theatrical notes in his *Diary*, refer to plays of Shakspere, which he deals with in a most amusing spirit of superiority: "September 29, 1662. To the King's Theatre, where we saw *Midsummer Night's Dream*, which I had never seen before, nor shall ever again, for it is the most insipid, ridiculous play that ever I saw in my life."

3. **Shakspere Scholarship, 1700-1750.**—In 1709 appeared the first critical edition of Shakspere's plays, that by Nicholas Rowe; he did something towards ascertaining the facts of Shakspere's life, and corrected a large number of the grosser errors of the folios. Rowe was succeeded as an editor by Pope in 1725; his six quarto volumes are more admirable from a bibliographical than from a literary point of view; his admiration of Shakspere was real, but his sympathy was imperfect; his emendations are in the spirit of

eighteenth century literature, not in the Elizabethan spirit. Theobald, the first hero of Pope's *Dunciad*, " piddling Tibbald ! " is infinitely a better editor than Pope ; if he amended the text often arbitrarily, on the other hand he first collated in anything like a scholarly manner the early copies of the plays. To his ingenuity as an emendator we owe the celebrated " 'a babbled of green fields," in the passage which tells of Falstaff's death. The merit of Theobald's edition, 1733, was recognised, and it sold largely. Hanmer's edition, remarkable like Pope's for its external splendour, followed in 1744, and three years later appeared that of Warburton. Warburton was learned, but arrogant, and treats Shakspere with the contemptuousness a harsh schoolmaster might exhibit toward a naughty urchin.

4. **Garrick.**—Such were the editions of the first half of the last century. The second half was a period of laborious scholarship and of industrious research after everything which could throw light on Shakspere's life or illustrate his writings. Between the two periods rose suddenly to eminence the great actor David Garrick. The immediate successors of Betterton were Booth, famous for his Othello, his rival Wilks, who played Hamlet, and Cibber, who appeared as his own Richard III., as Iago, and as Cardinal Wolsey. On October 19, 1741, at the theatre in Goodman's Fields, a young actor played for the first time Richard III. In a few weeks Garrick had become famous. The following year in Ireland, the hot summer and the young actor between them, produced what was named " The Garrick Fever." " That young man," said Pope, " never had his equal as an actor, and will never have a rival." In September, 1769, he assisted at a jubilee held in honour of Shakspere at Stratford-on-Avon. The Garrick fever had resulted in a Shakspere fever. Yet Garrick, it must be confessed, took unwarrantable liberties with the language and the plots of the plays, himself confessing that his adaptation of *Hamlet* was " the most impudent thing he ever did."

5. **Shakspere Scholarship, 1750-1800.**—The editions of the second half of the eighteenth century, begin with that of Dr. Johnson, 1765. Johnson saw some of the substantial excellencies of Shakspere, but his strong common sense was of a prosaic kind, and he often takes Shakspere to task for offences which only touch such prosaic common sense. As a moralist he was especially shocked at Shakspere's not rewarding virtue and punishing vice in the persons of his dramas with an orthodox regularity. Capell's edition in 1768, his "Notes and Various Readings," and his "School of Shakspere," were the labours of love of a very learned man, who obscured his merits by a strange and contorted style of writing. The work of Johnson was united with that of Steevens, five years later; Steevens was acute, witty, and sometimes brilliant, but conceited, utterly devoid of reverence for Shakspere, and without a true feeling for poetry. His adversary, Malone, was duller, but more industrious, more honest, and less vain. Steevens published a reprint of the quartos (1766), and *Six Old Plays* the originals on which Shakspere founded some of his dramas, in 1779. Malone's first edition appeared in 1790; it contained his own notes with those of his predecessors; and in 1803, 1813, and 1821, followed Variorum Editions, the last of these, called *Boswell's Malone*, being the most complete. Malone, unfortunately, had a very imperfect ear for verse.

6. **Ireland.**—Volumes of notes and criticism, of which perhaps the best known is Farmer's *Essay on the Learning of Shakspere*, became numerous in the second half of the eighteenth century. In the last decade of that century Shakspere scholars were startled by the announcement of the discovery of Shakspere autographs, letters, conundrums, confession of faith, and what not, of inestimable literary value; finally, a drama by Shakspere — *Vortigern* —was forthcoming, and was brought upon the stage by Kemble. The discoverer was a young man named W. H. Ireland, whose father, Samuel Ireland, was deceived, not himself a deceiver. Many people be-

SCIENCE PRIMERS.

UNDER THE JOINT EDITORSHIP OF

PROFESSORS HUXLEY, ROSCOE, AND BALFOUR STEWART.

"They are wonderfully clear and lucid in their instruction, simple in style and admirable in plan."—*Educational Times.*

The following are now ready:—

CHEMISTRY. By H. E. ROSCOE, F.R.S., Professor of Chemistry in Owens College, Manchester. 18mo. Illustrated. 1s. With Questions.

PHYSICS. By BALFOUR STEWART, F.R.S., Professor of Natural Philosophy in Owens College, Manchester. 18mo. Illustrated. 1s. With Questions.

PHYSICAL GEOGRAPHY. By A. GEIKIE, F.R.S., Murchison Professor of Geology and Mineralogy at Edinburgh. 18mo. Illustrated. 1s. With Questions.

GEOLOGY. By Professor GEIKIE, F.R.S. With numerous Illustrations. 18mo. 1s.

PHYSIOLOGY. By MICHAEL FOSTER, M.D., F.R.S. With numerous Illustrations. 18mo. 1s.

ASTRONOMY. By J. NORMAN LOCKYER, F.R.S. With numerous Illustrations. 18mo. 1s.

BOTANY. By Sir J. D. HOOKER, K.C.S.I., C.B., President of the Royal Society. Illustrated. 18mo. 1s.

LOGIC. By Professor STANLEY JEVONS, F.R.S. 18mo. 1s.

POLITICAL ECONOMY. By Professor JEVONS, F.R.S. 18mo. 1s.

INTRODUCTORY. By Prof. HUXLEY, F.R.S.
[*Preparing with others.*

MACMILLAN AND CO., LONDON.

HISTORY AND LITERATURE PRIMERS.

Edited by JOHN RICHARD GREEN,
Author of "A Short History of the English People."

In 18mo, cloth, price 1s. each.

HOMER. By the Right Hon. W. E. GLADSTONE.

ENGLISH GRAMMAR EXERCISES. By R. MORRIS, LL.D., and H. C. BOWEN.

ENGLISH GRAMMAR. By R. MORRIS, LL.D.

HISTORY OF ROME. By M. CREIGHTON, M.A. With Maps.

HISTORY OF GREECE. By C. A. FYFFE, M.A. With Maps.

ENGLISH LITERATURE. By the Rev. STOPFORD BROOKE, M.A.

HISTORY OF EUROPE. By E. A. FREEMAN, D.C.L., LL.D. With Maps.

GREEK ANTIQUITIES. By J. P. MAHAFFY, M.A. Illustrated.

ROMAN ANTIQUITIES. By Prof. A. S. WILKINS. Illustrated.

CLASSICAL GEOGRAPHY. By H. F. TOZER.

GEOGRAPHY. By GEORGE GROVE, F.R.G.S. With Maps.

CHILDREN'S TREASURY OF LYRICAL POETRY. By F. T. PALGRAVE. In Two Parts. 1s. each.

SHAKSPERE. By Prof. DOWDEN.

PHILOLOGY. By J. PEILE, M.A.

GREEK LITERATURE. By Prof. JEBB, M.A.

FRANCE. By CHARLOTTE M. YONGE.

GEOGRAPHY OF GREAT BRITAIN AND IRELAND. By JOHN RICHARD GREEN and ALICE STOPFORD GREEN. With Maps.

ENGLISH COMPOSITION. By Professor NICHOL.

MACMILLAN AND CO., LONDON.

www.ingramcontent.com/pod-product-compliance
Lightning Source LLC
Chambersburg PA
CBHW030258170426
43202CB00009B/797